SUGAR FREE
for everyone

Published in 2017 by Bounty Books based on materials licensed to it by Bauer Media Books, Australia.

Bauer Media Books are published by
Bauer Media Pty Limited
54 Park St, Sydney; GPO Box 4088,
Sydney, NSW 2001 Australia
phone +61 2 9282 8618; fax +61 2 9126 3702
www.awwcookbooks.com.au

PUBLISHER
Jo Runciman

EDITORIAL & FOOD DIRECTOR
Sophia Young

DIRECTOR OF SALES, MARKETING & RIGHTS
Brian Cearnes

EDITORIAL DIRECTOR-AT-LARGE
Pamela Clark

CREATIVE DIRECTOR
Hannah Blackmore

DESIGNER
Jeannel Cunanan

MANAGING EDITOR
Stephanie Kistner

JUNIOR EDITOR
Amanda Lees

FOOD EDITORS
Sophia Young, Kathleen Davis

OPERATIONS MANAGER
David Scotto

PRINTED IN CHINA
by Leo Paper Products Ltd.

PUBLISHED AND DISTRIBUTED in the
United Kingdom by Bounty Books,
a division of Octopus Publishing Group Ltd
Carmelite House
50 Victoria Embankment
London, EC4Y 0DZ
United Kingdom
info@octopus-publishing.co.uk;
www.octopusbooks.co.uk

INTERNATIONAL FOREIGN LANGUAGE RIGHTS
Brian Cearnes, Bauer Media Books
bcearnes@bauer-media.com.au

A catalogue record for this book is
available from the British Library.
ISBN: 978-0-7537-3258-8

THE AUSTRALIAN
Women's Weekly

SUGAR FREE
For everyone

Bounty
BOOKS

CONTENTS

Sugar-Free Living 6

Sugar Alternatives 8

POWER UP 10

MAKE *and* SAVE 44

LUNCH OR DINNER 82

QUICK FIXES 124

SWEET STUFF 168

Glossary 234

Conversion chart 237

Index 238

SUGAR—FREE living

The recipes in this book are free from added refined sugars, including sucrose (table sugar). However, unrefined sugars and sugars naturally present in whole foods are included.

A quick read of the ingredient list on the back of many food products these days reveals the variety of forms and unexpected places sugar crops up. You will see syrups, including rice malt syrup (brown rice syrup), molasses, agave syrup, treacle, cane juice, coconut sugar, rapadura; then perhaps less well known forms of sugar — dextrose, glucose, sucrose, maltodextrin and maltose.

NATURAL SWEETNERS

Of all the sweetners, honey, if chosen wisely, is one of the most natural. It can be from a single source or a blend from multiple sources. Honey has been a part of human diets since hunter-gatherer days. Maple syrup is also a sugar, and like honey is not as refined as most others. From a cooking perspective both maple syrup and honey add a delicious flavour to recipes. Nevertheless be aware, they are still sugars, and if you have chosen to follow a truly sugar-free diet you'll need to give them a miss.

Natural alternatives to sucrose include sorbitol (commonly used in sugar-free gums and mints), xylitol, stevia or monk fruit (sold as norbu). These are all naturally sweet, provide fewer kilojoules, do not raise blood sugar levels and are tooth friendly. For more information on these and other alternatives, see page 9.

SUGARS iN FRUIT & VEGETABLES

In the quest for better health via improved eating patterns it is important to understand the difference between naturally occurring sugars in fruit, and even vegetables, and those that are added to food. Fruits and vegetables are rich in fibre and contain a host of antioxidants, vitamins, minerals and phytonutrients that are beneficial to our health. They have an essential place in our diet. It is also improtant to eat from a wide array of plant sources rather than making mono choices to guarantee better nutrition.

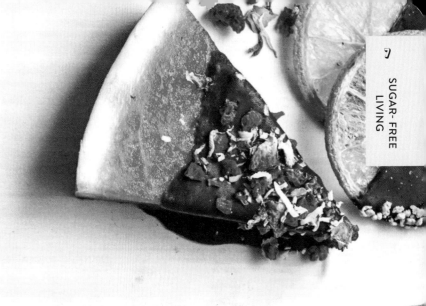

TAKE A BIG PICTURE LOOK

A word of caution however, is that
you don't become so fixated on sugar
that you forget to step back and look
at your total diet. There are many
aspects of diet that are important,
and blaming just one thing is
dangerous as it blinds us to other,
just as important, aspects. Instead,
focus on reducing or, if you like,
completely cutting out foods with
added refined sugars — starting with
the obvious no-nos such as lollies,
biscuits, cakes and sugar-sweetened
soft drinks, as they contain little
or no nutritional value.

WHOLESOME FOOD

The recipes in this book take a
more holistic approach to food.
The focus is on eating whole foods
from all food groups and choosing
wisely within them. We've covered
all manner of every day dishes where
refined sugars are often unnecessarily
present — from the obvious baked
goodies to the not-so-obvious
marinades, salad dressings and
savoury sauces. Using unrefined
alternatives and wholefoods we've
developed scrumptious breakfasts,
main meals, make and save items,
and sweet treats the entire family
will love — they won't even notice
what's missing.

Swap this →	FOR THAT
TOASTED GRANOLA	ROLLED OATS
DIET MAYONNAISE	FULL-FAT MAYONNAISE
ORANGE JUICE	WHOLE ORANGES
FRUIT YOGHURTS	NATURAL YOGHURT
WHITE BREAD	WHOLEGRAIN BREAD
MUESLI BARS	A HANDFUL OF NUTS
TOMATO SAUCE (KETCHUP)	MUSTARD
BOUGHT DRESSINGS	OLIVE OIL & LEMON JUICE
COMMERCIAL CHAI LATTE MIXES	REGULAR TEA
ENERGY DRINKS	MINERAL WATER
DRINKING CHOCOLATE	DUTCH COCOA
MILK CHOCOLATE	85% DARK CHOCOLATE
PASTA SAUCE	PASSATA

COCONUT SUGAR

Coconut sugar (coconut palm sugar) is not made from coconuts, but from the sap of the blossoms of the coconut palm tree. The sap is collected and then boiled to evaporate the water content, leaving a sugar that looks a little like raw or light brown sugar with a similar caramel flavour. While it has the same amount of kilojoules as regular white sugar, but on the plus side it does contain some trace minerals.

RICE MALT SYRUP

Rice malt syrup (brown rice syrup) is made by cooking brown rice flour with enzymes to break down the starch into sugars. The mixture is then filtered and the water removed to give a thick, sweet syrup with a mild taste. It is available from most major supermarkets and health food stores. Rice malt syrup is fructose-free and is a popular vegan alternative to honey.

AGAVE SYRUP

Agave syrup (agave nectar) is a sweetener produced from the agave plant (a succulent with thick fleshy leaves) native to South Africa and Mexico. It has a low GI due to the high percentage of fructose present, which may be harmful if consumed in high quantities. Sweeter and slightly thinner than honey, it is a suitable vegan substitute for honey. It is available from supermarkets.

SUGAR Alternatives

YACON SYRUP

From the roots of the yacon plant, contains a high percentage of fructooligosaccharides which aren't digested so it has only a third of the calories of sugar. It is not suitable for cooking.

BARLEY MALT SYRUP

A dark brown, thick unrefined syrup made from sprouted (malted) barley, with a "malty" flavour. It is less sweet than honey or regular sugar and is low in glucose, fructose and sucrose.

STEVIA

Made from the leave of the stevia plant; highly refined to produce a sugar-like mixture that has a minimal effect on blood glucose levels and has no kilojoules.

RAW HONEY

Honey is one of the most natural sweeteners. Pure floral honeys have a low GI, but cheaper, blended honeys tend to be high. For a low GI honey look for Yellow Box, Stringy Bark, Red Gum, Iron Bark or Eucalypt.

PURE MAPLE SYRUP

Pure maple syrup is the concentrated sap of the maple tree, whereas maple-flavoured syrups are usually just processed glucose syrup with added flavourings. Real maple syrup is much tastier and contains significant amounts of nutrients and antioxidant compounds. It has a low GI, making it a good choice for blood glucose control.

POWER UP

BEETROOT AND CACAO PANCAKES WITH RASPBERRY CHIA JAM

PREP + COOK TIME 1 HOUR 15 MINUTES (+ REFRIGERATION) SERVES 4

- 2 small beetroots (200g), peeled
- 1 cup (250ml) coconut and brown rice milk blend (see tips)
- 2 eggs, beaten lightly
- 2 tablespoons pure maple syrup
- 1½ cups (225g) self-raising flour
- ¼ cup (25g) cacao powder
- 2 tablespoons cacao nibs
- 1 tablespoon coconut oil, at room temperature
- ⅔ cup (190g) unsweetened coconut or Greek-style yoghurt
- 1 tablespoon cacao nibs, extra
- 125g fresh raspberries

RASPBERRY CHIA JAM

- 1 cup (150g) frozen raspberries, thawed
- 2 tablespoons water
- 2 tablespoons white chia seeds
- 2 tablespoons rice malt syrup

1 Preheat oven to 200°C/400°F.
2 Make raspberry chia jam.
3 Wrap beetroot individually in foil, place on an oven tray; roast for 40 minutes or until tender. Cool; chop coarsely.
4 Blend beetroot to a smooth puree; transfer to a bowl. Measure ½ cup of puree, return measured puree to blender with milk; blend until smooth. Add egg, maple syrup, sifted flour and cacao; process until a smooth batter just forms. Transfer to a jug; stir in cacao nibs.
5 Working in batches, heat 1 teaspoon of the coconut oil in a medium frying pan over medium heat. Add ⅓ cup batter; repeat with another ⅓ cup batter, cook pancakes for 2 minutes or until bubbles appear. Turn pancakes; cook for a further minute or until cooked through. Repeat with remaining coconut oil and batter to make eight pancakes in total.
6 Serve pancakes topped with yoghurt, raspberry chia jam, extra cacao nibs and raspberries.

RASPBERRY CHIA JAM

Blend or process raspberries and the water until pureed. Pour into a small bowl; stir through chia seeds and syrup. Cover; refrigerate for at least 1 hour or until thickened to a jam-like consistency.

TIPS You may need to add 1-2 tablespoons of water to help the beetroot blend to a smooth puree. If you have leftover puree, combine it with Greek-style yoghurt, fresh herbs, garlic and a pinch of cumin for an instant beetroot dip. We used Coco Quench, a blend of coconut milk and brown rice milk, available from selected supermarkets and health food stores. Substitute with your favourite non-dairy milk or, if preferred, regular milk. You can use coconut sugar, honey or maple syrup to sweeten the pancakes.

TIP You can melt
the coconut oil in
a microwave;
alternatively, sit a
bowl of coconut oil
in a bowl filled with
a little boiling
water, then stir
until melted.

* This array of seeds and nuts,
plus a healthy dose of kale, offers
a wide spectrum of nutrients.

DAILY GREENS GREENOLA

PREP + COOK TIME **40 MINUTES (+ COOLING)** SERVES **8**

- ⅓ bunch green kale (100g)
- ½ teaspoon melted coconut oil
- 2 teaspoons ground cinnamon
- 1 cup (140g) sunflower seeds
- ⅓ cup (55g) white chia seeds
- 1½ cups (300g) pepitas (pumpkin seed kernels)
- 1 cup (140g) slivered almonds
- 1 cup (170g) raw buckwheat
- 3 teaspoons spirulina powder
- 1 teaspoon pure vanilla extract
- ¼ cup (60ml) melted coconut oil, extra
- ¼ cup (60ml) pure maple syrup

1 Preheat oven to 180°C/350°F. Line three large oven trays with baking paper.
2 Tear kale leaves from stems; discard stems. Place kale on one oven tray, drizzle with coconut oil and sprinkle with 1 teaspoon of the cinnamon; massage oil and cinnamon into kale. Bake kale for 15 minutes, stirring halfway through, or until crisp. When cool enough to handle, using your hands, crush kale finely.
3 Meanwhile, place seeds, almonds and buckwheat in a large bowl; sprinkle with spirulina and remaining cinnamon. Stir vanilla into extra coconut oil, drizzle over seed mixture with maple syrup; toss well to coat. Spread mixture evenly over remaining oven trays.
4 Roast for 20 minutes, stirring halfway, or until nuts are golden. Cool. Combine crushed kale with seed mixture.

TRY THIS for breakfast with ⅓ cup almond milk, half a thinly sliced pear and half a kiwifruit. Alternatively, keep a jar handy on your desk at work to ward off the 3pm slump.

KEEPS Store greenola in an airtight container in the pantry for up to 1 month.

BONE BROTH SMOOTHIES

✳ The concept of including broth (stock) in a smoothie might at first seem
odd, or even unpleasant. Freezing neutralises the taste of the broth, adding
no discernible meat taste to the smoothie. Bone broth advocates believe the
natural occurring gelatine (collagen), amino acids and minerals in homemade
broths contribute to good gut health. While there are no reliable studies
to back this up, drinking broths is an age-old practice in many cultures.
If you decide to skip the bone broth, they still make delicious fruit smoothies.

RASPBERRY AND CACAO SMOOTHIE

PREP TIME 5 MINUTES (+ FREEZING) SERVES 2

- 270ml (8½ ounces) canned coconut milk
- 1 cup (150g) frozen raspberries
- 2 frozen beef bone broth ice cubes (see page 61)
- 1 tablespoon pure maple syrup
- 1 teaspoon cacao powder
- frozen rapberries, extra, to serve

1 Blend all ingredients in a blender until smooth.
2 Pour between two small glasses; top with extra raspberries to serve.

MANGO, MAPLE AND MESQUITE SMOOTHIE

PREP + COOK TIME 5 MINUTES (+ FREEZING) SERVES 2

- 1 cup (250ml) almond milk
- 1 large mango (430g), peeled, chopped, frozen
- 2 frozen beef bone broth ice cubes (see page 61)
- 1 tablespoon pure maple syrup
- 1 teaspoon mesquite powder (see page 127)
- sliced mango, extra, to serve

1 Blend all ingredients in a blender until smooth.
2 Pour between two small glasses; top with sliced mango to serve.

TIPS Take your pick as to how you want to introduce the vanilla flavour to this porridge. Vanilla beans provide the purest flavour and the bean itself can be reused if it is rinsed and dried. Alternatively, a more economical option is to use 1 teaspoon vanilla extract. However, it does contain a trace amount of sugar, but really nothing one should be too bothered about. Another option is vanilla bean powder from health food stores, which is both the ground bean and seeds; vanilla in this form tends to be less potent.

WARMING QUINOA PORRIDGE

PREP + COOK TIME **15 MINUTES** SERVES **4**

- 1 litre (4 cups) soy milk or nut milk
- 3 granny smith apples (450g), grated coarsely
- 1 vanilla bean, split lengthways, seeds scraped (see tips)
- 125g (4 ounces) blueberries
- ¾ cup (70g) quinoa flakes
- ¼ cup (50g) black chia seeds
- ⅓ cup (140g) unsweetened coconut or other vegan yoghurt
- ⅓ cup (45g) skinless roasted hazelnuts, chopped coarsely
- ⅓ cup (80ml) pure maple syrup or honey

1 Place milk, apple, vanilla bean and seeds in a medium saucepan over low heat; cook for 5 minutes or until milk is almost boiling and apple is softened.

2 Lightly crush half the blueberries, add to the pan with quinoa flakes and chia seeds; cook, stirring, for 5 minutes or until thickened. Remove vanilla bean, reserve for another use (see tips).

3 Serve porridge topped with yoghurt, hazelnuts and remaining blueberries. Drizzle with maple syrup.

SWAP OUT apples for pears, blueberries for strawberries and hazelnuts for almonds, for a different take on this porridge.

BIG BEAUTIFUL BREAKFAST BOWL

PREP + COOK TIME **35 MINUTES** SERVES **4**

- 1 cup (200g) quinoa, rinsed
- 1¾ cups (430ml) water
- 4 eggs, shells rinsed well
- 170g (5½ ounces) asparagus, trimmed, halved crossways
- 1 tablespoon extra virgin olive oil
- 2 tablespoons pistachio dukkah (see tips)
- 300g (9½ ounces) baby spinach, washed well
- 1 avocado (250g), sliced thinly

TAHINI DRESSING

- ¼ cup (70g) unhulled tahini
- 1 tablespoon extra virgin olive oil
- ¼ cup (60ml) lemon juice
- 2 tablespoons water

1 Place quinoa and the water in a saucepan; bring to the boil. Reduce heat to low; simmer, covered, for 12 minutes or until water is absorbed and quinoa is tender. Remove from heat; stand, covered for 5 minutes.

2 Meanwhile, cook eggs in a saucepan of boiling salted water for 6 minutes for soft-boiled or until cooked to your liking. Remove with a slotted spoon; cool under running water. Return water to the boil. Cook asparagus for 3 minutes; drain. Cut asparagus in half diagonally.

3 Meanwhile, make tahini dressing.

4 Peel eggs, place in a bowl; drizzle with oil. Place dukkah in a small bowl; roll eggs in dukkah to coat.

5 Serve quinoa with asparagus, spinach, avocado and eggs; drizzle with tahini dressing and season to taste.

TAHINI DRESSING
Whisk all the ingredients in a small bowl until combined and emulsified; season to taste.

TIPS Dukkah is available in different forms from supermarkets and delis; any variety is suitable for this recipe. Alternatively, you can roll the eggs in toasted sesame seeds mixed with a little ground cumin. Mornings can be a rush, so have all your ingredients weighed out and ready to go. If you want to speed things up further, make the tahini dressing and cook the eggs the night before; store, separately in the refrigerator.

BANANA AND CINNAMON PIKELETS WITH PAN-FRIED GRANOLA

PREP + COOK TIME **20 MINUTES** SERVES **4**

Get a head start on this breakfast by making the pan-fried granola a couple of days ahead; cool and store in an airtight jar for up to 2 weeks.

- 2 medium overripe bananas (400g), mashed
- 4 eggs
- ¼ cup (60ml) almond milk
- ½ teaspoon ground cinnamon
- ½ cup (75g) self-raising flour
- ½ teaspoon bicarbonate of soda (baking soda)
- 2 tablespoons coconut oil
- 2 medium bananas (400g), sliced lengthways
- ⅓ cup (95g) unsweetened coconut yoghurt
- 2 tablespoons fresh passionfruit pulp

PAN-FRIED GRANOLA

- ½ teaspoon coconut oil
- 2 tablespoons coconut flakes
- 2 tablespoons pecans, chopped coarsely
- 2 tablespoons pepitas (pumpkin seed kernels)
- ¼ teaspoon ground cinnamon
- 1 teaspoon pure maple syrup

1 Make pan-fried granola.

2 Whisk banana, eggs and milk in a medium bowl until well combined. Sift over cinnamon, flour and soda; fold to combine.

3 Heat 2 teaspoons of the coconut oil in a large frying pan over medium heat. Working in batches, add four 2-tablespoon quantities of the batter; cook for 1 minute or until edge of each pikelet has set and bubbles appear on the surface. Turn pikelets using a spatula; cook for a further 30 seconds or until cooked through. Transfer to a plate; cover to keep warm. Repeat three more times with remaining coconut oil and batter to make 16 pikelets in total.

4 Top piklets with sliced banana, yoghurt and passionfruit. Serve sprinkled with pan-fried granola.

PAN-FRIED GRANOLA

Heat coconut oil in a small frying pan over medium-high heat. Cook coconut flakes, pecans, pepitas and cinnamon, stirring, for 2 minutes or until lightly toasted. Add syrup; cook, stirring for 1 minute or until granola is golden. Remove from pan; cool.

TURMERIC CHIA BREAKFAST PUDDINGS

PREP + COOK TIME **20 MINUTES (+ REFRIGERATION)** MAKES **6**

- 3 cups (750ml) coconut milk
- 1 cinnamon stick
- 1½ teaspoons grated fresh turmeric
- 1½ teaspoons grated fresh ginger
- ¼ cup (90g) honey
- ⅓ cup (55g) white chia seeds
- 500g (1 pound) unsweetened coconut yoghurt
- 2 medium bananas (300g), sliced thinly
- ½ cup (40g) coconut flakes, toasted

TURMERIC & PASSIONFRUIT HONEY

- ⅓ cup (115g) honey
- 1 teaspoon grated fresh turmeric
- 1 passionfruit, pulp removed

1 Place coconut milk, cinnamon, turmeric and ginger in a small saucepan, bring to a simmer over medium heat; cook for 5 minutes to infuse milk with spices.
2 Strain milk mixture through a fine sieve over a small heatproof bowl; discard solids. Stir honey and chia seeds into hot infused milk; cover bowl with a clean tea towel. Refrigerate for 30 minutes or until thickened.
3 Meanwhile, make turmeric and passionfruit honey.
4 Divide one-quarter of the chia pudding among six 300ml jars or 1-cup (250ml) glasses. Top with one-quarter of the coconut yoghurt. Press half the banana slices in a ring around the inside of the jar. Repeat layering with remaining chia pudding and yoghurt to create four layers of each. Top puddings with remaining banana and coconut flakes; drizzle with turmeric and passionfruit honey.

TURMERIC & PASSIONFRUIT HONEY

Place all ingredients in a small saucepan; bring to the boil. Reduce heat to medium; simmer for 1 minute to infuse. Cool to room temperature.

SWAP OUT the fresh grated spices with ground spices; use 2 teaspoons ground cinnamon, 1½ teaspoons ground turmeric and 1 teaspoon ground ginger. You could also use dairy milk and yoghurt instead of coconut, if preferred. If you are not a fan of spices, simply stir in 1 teaspoon pure vanilla extract and 1 teaspoon finely grated orange or lemon rind into the milk.

KEEPS Store layered puddings in the fridge for up to 2 days, or the un-layered chia mixture in the fridge for up to 1 week.

TIP Make the chia base mixture on the weekend, then layer the mixture each morning in jars, either with the banana and yoghurt in our recipe, or with the fruit of your choice, for a quick and easy breakfast to almost see you through the week.

TIP To prepare kale, tear the leaves from the tough stalks; discard stalks. Coarsely shred the kale leaves.

PEA AND KALE FRITTERS WITH HOT-SMOKED SALMON

PREP + COOK TIME **35 MINUTES** SERVES **4**

- 1 cup (150g) buckwheat flour
- 1 cup (280g) Greek-style yoghurt
- 4 eggs
- 3 cups (360g) frozen peas, thawed
- 6 cups (170g) loosely packed shredded kale leaves (see tip)
- ¼ cup (60ml) extra virgin olive oil
- 1 lemon (140g), rind finely grated, cut into wedges
- 2 x 150g (4½-ounce) hot-smoked salmon fillets, flaked into large pieces
- ¼ cup finely chopped fresh chives
- ¼ cup finely chopped fresh flat-leaf parsley

1 Preheat oven to 150°C/300°F.

2 Whisk buckwheat flour, ½ cup of the yoghurt and eggs in a large bowl; season well. Stir in peas and kale until well combined.

3 Heat 1 tablespoon of the oil in a large frying pan over medium-high heat. Add four heaped ⅓ cupfuls of fritter mixture to pan; cook for 3 minutes each side or until golden and cooked through. Transfer to an oven tray, cover loosely with foil; keep warm on the lowest oven shelf. Repeat twice more with remaining oil and fritter mixture to make 12 fritters.

4 Whisk remaining yoghurt with lemon rind; season.

5 Top fritters with yoghurt mixture, salmon and herbs. Serve with lemon wedges.

STRAWBERRY, RICOTTA AND BASIL BRUSCHETTA WITH BITTER HONEY

PREP + COOK TIME **35 MINUTES (+ STANDING & REFRIGERATION)** SERVES **4**

You will need to begin this recipe a day ahead.

- 3 cups (750ml) full-cream milk
- 300ml pouring cream
- ½ teaspoon salt flakes
- ¼ cup (60ml) lemon juice
- 500g (1 pound) small strawberries, trimmed, halved
- ¼ cup (60ml) sugar-free balsamic vinegar or red wine vinegar
- 8 thick slices (600g) wholegrain sourdough, cut on the diagonal
- 1 cup small fresh basil leaves

BITTER HONEY

- 1½ tablespoons roasted dandelion and chicory root blend (see tips)
- 2 teaspoons instant coffee granules
- 1 cup (350g) honey
- ¼ cup (60ml) water

1 Combine milk, cream and salt in a 2 litre (8 cup) heavy-based saucepan over medium heat. Cook, stirring occasionally using a wooden spoon, for 10 minutes or until just below simmering point, or a digital thermometer reads 85°C (185°F).

2 Remove from heat and stir through lemon juice. Stand for 30 minutes or until solid curds form. Strain mixture through a muslin-lined sieve over a bowl. Refrigerate for 2 hours or until curds and liquid whey are separated. Reserve whey (see tips). (Makes 2 cups (475g) ricotta and 2 cups (500ml) whey.)

3 Meanwhile, make bitter honey.

4 Transfer drained curds to a large bowl, whisk until smooth; season to taste. Transfer to an airtight container; refrigerate overnight to set.

5 Place strawberries and vinegar in a large glass bowl, season with freshly ground black pepper; stir to combine. Cover tightly with plastic wrap; leave in a warm place for 1 hour. Stir again before serving; drain.

6 Heat a barbecue or chargrill plate on high. Grill sourdough for 2 minutes each side or until grill marks appear.

7 Serve ricotta spread on toast, topped with strawberries and basil; drizzle with bitter honey.

BITTER HONEY

Using a mortar and pestle or a spice grinder, grind dandelion and chicory blend and coffee granules to form a coarse powder. Place honey and the water in a small saucepan. Sift over dandelion and chicory mixture; bring to the boil, whisking occasionally. Simmer for 3 minutes. Leave to cool for 15 minutes before skimming surface; transfer to a sterilised jar (see page 236). Leave to cool at room temperature.

TRY THIS

Bitter honey drizzled over soft cheese on crispbread.
Ricotta spread on rosemary and cacao crackers (see page 65) or cheesy parsnip teff bread (see page 74) or as a substitute for goat's curd in the roast beetroot and buckwheat risotto (see page 84).

KEEPS Store bitter honey in the pantry for up to 1 month. Store ricotta in an airtight container in the fridge for up to 1 week.

TIPS When making ricotta, use the drained liquid (whey) in your next batch of bread or pizza dough instead of water or use a few spoonfuls to jump-start the lacto-fermentation process when making pickles. Roasted dandelion and chicory root blend is a caffeine-free coffee substitute available from health food stores.

FIVE-MINUTE HUNGER BUSTER

BLUEBERRY, ORANGE & OAT HUNGER BUSTER

COFFEE & COCONUT HUNGER BUSTER

BANANA & TAHINI HUNGER BUSTER

HUNGER BUSTERS

FIVE-MINUTE HUNGER BUSTER

PREP + COOK TIME
5 MINUTES SERVES **1**

Lightly grease a 1½ cup microwave-safe mug. Combine ¼ cup wholemeal spelt flour, 2 tablespoons LSA, ½ teaspoon baking powder and ¼ teaspoon ground cinnamon in a small bowl. Whisk 2 tablespoons melted coconut butter, 1 egg, 2 tablespoons milk of choice, ½ teaspoon pure vanilla extract and 2 teaspoons pure maple syrup in the mug. Stir in dry ingredients. Place in the centre of the microwave tray. Microwave on HIGH (100%) for 2 minutes or until just cooked. Serve immediately, topped with butter, extra pure maple syrup and a pinch of ground cinnamon.

TIPS Coconut butter is the ground flesh of the coconut; you can find it in health food stores. Substitute coconut oil or butter. LSA is a ground mixture of linseeds, sunflower seeds and almonds available from supermarkets. You can also use dairy-free milk, if you prefer.

BLUEBERRY, ORANGE & OAT HUNGER BUSTER

PREP + COOK TIME
5 MINUTES SERVES **1**

Lightly grease a 1½ cup microwave-safe mug. Combine ¼ cup wholemeal spelt flour, 2 tablespoons quick oats, ½ teaspoon baking powder and ¼ teaspoon ground cinnamon in a small bowl. Whisk 2 tablespoons melted coconut butter, 1 egg, 2 tablespoons milk of choice, 1 teaspoon finely grated orange rind, ½ teaspoon pure vanilla extract and 2 teaspoons pure maple syrup in the mug. Stir in dry ingredients and 2 tablespoons frozen blueberries; top with an extra 1 tablespoon frozen blueberries. Place in the centre of the microwave tray. Microwave on HIGH (100%) for 2 minutes or until just cooked. Serve immediately, topped with unsweetened coconut yoghurt and extra orange rind.

COFFEE & COCONUT HUNGER BUSTER

PREP + COOK TIME
5 MINUTES SERVES **1**

Lightly grease a 1½ cup microwave-safe mug. Pit 2 fresh dates; chop coarsely. Combine ¼ cup wholemeal spelt flour, 2 tablespoons desiccated coconut, 2½ tablespoons melted coconut butter, 1 egg, 2 tablespoons milk of choice, 1 teaspoon instant coffee granules, ½ teaspoon pure vanilla extract and 2 teaspoons pure maple syrup in the mug. Stir in the dry ingredients and three-quarters of the dates. Top with remaining dates. Place in the centre of the microwave tray. Microwave on HIGH (100%) for 2 minutes or until just cooked. Serve immediately topped with extra pure maple syrup.

TIP You can melt the coconut butter in the mug in the microwave for 30 seconds.

BANANA & TAHINI HUNGER BUSTER

PREP + COOK TIME
5 MINUTES SERVES **1**

Lightly grease a 1½ cup microwave-safe mug. Chop ½ small ripe banana finely. Combine ¼ cup wholemeal spelt flour, 2 tablespoons LSA, ½ teaspoon baking powder and ¼ teaspoon ground cinnamon in a small bowl. Whisk 2 tablespoons hulled tahini, 1 egg, 2 tablespoons milk of choice, ½ teaspoon pure vanilla extract and 2 teaspoons pure maple syrup in the mug. Stir in the dry ingredients and three-quarters of the banana. Place in the centre of the microwave tray. Microwave on HIGH (100%) for 2 minutes or until just cooked. Serve immediately topped with unsweetened coconut yoghurt, remaining banana, sliced thinly, and extra cinnamon.

✳ Place this show-stopping brekkie pudding
in the centre of the table at brunch as the main
attraction for family or guests to help themselves.

BERRY AND FIG WEEKEND BREKKIE PUDDING

PREP + COOK TIME **40 MINUTES** SERVES 6

- 40g (1½ ounces) butter, softened
- 1 vanilla bean (see tips)
- ½ cup (125ml) water
- 1 cup (230g) fresh dates, pitted
- 2 tablespoons ground turmeric
- 2 tablespoons ground cinnamon
- 5cm (2-inch) piece fresh ginger, chopped coarsely
- 1 cup (120g) almond meal
- 400ml can coconut cream
- 1½ teaspoons baking powder
- ¼ cup (35g) self-raising flour
- 8 eggs
- ¼ cup (90g) raw honey
- 3 medium fresh figs (180g), cut into wedges
- 150g (4½ ounces) fresh raspberries
- 150g (4½ ounces) fresh blackberries
- 1 cup (150g) fresh cherries, pitted
- 1½ cups (420g) unsweetened coconut yoghurt

1 Preheat oven to 200°C/400°F. Grease a 1.5 litre (6-cup) capacity baking dish with half the butter.

2 Split vanilla bean lengthways, scrape seeds from halves, using the tip of a knife. Process vanilla seeds, the water, dates, turmeric, cinnamon, ginger, almond meal, coconut cream, baking powder and flour until smooth.

3 Whisk eggs in a large bowl until light and frothy. Add turmeric mixture to egg; stir gently to combine. Pour into baking dish.

4 Bake pudding for 25 minutes or until risen and firm. Remove and cool for 15 minutes.

5 Meanwhile, heat remaining butter and the honey in a large frying pan over medium heat; cook figs for 2 minutes each side or until light golden. Add berries and cherries; cook for 1 minute or until berries release their juices.

6 Spread coconut yoghurt over pudding. Top with warm fruit and pan juices.

TIPS Place the leftover vanilla bean in a zip-top bag and save for another use. Use to flavour roasted fruit or for a decadent hot chocolate, or cut into shorter lengths and slip into a jar of muesli to infuse with a vanilla flavour. To make this dairy-free, use cacao butter instead of regular butter.

TIPS Make a batch of kitchari and store it in an airtight container in the fridge for up to 3 days for quick breakfasts throughout the week. Reheat on the stove or in the microwave. Ghee is clarified butter and can be found in tubs alongside butter in the refrigerator section or in jars in the Indian section of supermarkets.

✳ Kitchari is a nourishing traditional Indian mix of rice, lentils and vegetables. While these ingredients may not seem like typical breakfast fare, they have many benefits. Contributing phytochemicals, dietary fibre and protein, which help keep blood sugar levels stable, you'll last the distance until lunch time.

RED LENTIL KITCHARI

PREP + COOK TIME **35 MINUTES** SERVES **4**

- 1 tablespoon ghee (see tips) or olive oil
- 1 small brown onion (80g), chopped finely
- 1 medium carrot (70g), diced finely
- 2 small tomatoes (180g), diced
- 1 teaspoon yellow mustard seeds
- 1 teaspoon cumin seeds
- ½ teaspoon ground turmeric
- 1 cup (200g) brown basmati rice
- ½ cup (100g) dried red lentils
- 3 cups (750ml) water
- Greek-style yoghurt, coriander (cilantro) and lime wedges, to serve

1 Heat ghee in a medium saucepan over medium-high heat. Cook onion, carrot and tomato, stirring, for 3 minutes or until softened. Add spices; cook, stirring, for 1 minute or until fragrant. Add rice and lentils; stir to coat in spices. Add the water; bring to boil. Reduce heat to low; cook, covered, stirring occasionally, for 20 minutes or until rice is tender and lentils are soft. Season to taste.

2 Serve kitchari with yoghurt, coriander and lime wedges and season with freshly ground black pepper, if you like.

※ Ayurveda is an ancient Indian health practice
incorporating medicine, yoga and diet. An Ayurvedic
diet encourages eating from a wide range of food
sources, incorporating six principle tastes: sour,
salty, pungent, sweet, bitter and astringent.

AYURVEDIC AMARANTH PORRIDGE

PREP + COOK TIME **45 MINUTES (+ STANDING)** SERVES **2**

You will need to start this recipe a day ahead.

- 1 cup (200g) amaranth (see tips)
- 1 cup (250ml) coconut milk
- 1 cup (250ml) water
- ½ teaspoon ground cardamom
- ½ teaspoon ground cinnamon
- 2 fresh dates, pitted, chopped
- 1 vanilla bean, split lengthways, seeds scraped

- 2 teaspoons pepitas (pumpkin seed kernels)
- 2 teaspoons sunflower seeds
- 2 teaspoons black sesame seeds
- 2 tablespoons coconut milk, extra
- 1 tablespoon pure maple syrup
- frozen raspberries, to serve, optional

1 Place amaranth in a medium bowl with enough water to cover; stand overnight.
Drain amaranth, rinse under cold water; drain well.
2 Place amaranth, coconut milk, the water, spices, dates, vanilla seeds and
bean in a medium saucepan; bring to the boil. Reduce heat to low; simmer gently,
stirring frequently, for 25 minutes or until amaranth is no longer gritty.
If the porridge dries out, add a little extra water. Discard vanilla bean.
3 Meanwhile, heat a small frying pan over medium heat; cook seeds, stirring
for 2 minutes or until toasted. Remove from pan; cool.
4 Divide porridge between bowls; drizzle with extra coconut milk and the maple
syrup. Serve topped with toasted seeds and raspberries.

TIPS While sometimes referred to as a grain, strictly speaking amaranth is a nutritious gluten-free seed with a nutty taste. It can be found at large supermarkets and health food stores. It is important to soak the amaranth overnight in cold water, otherwise the mixture will be gritty and the cooking time will double.

TIPS If all you can find are white dragon fruit (pitaya), use those instead and add 1 small beetroot (100g) when blending all the ingredients for a similar vivid pink colour, if you like. Dragon fruit is generally not found at supermarkets, but is available from independent greengrocers.

* Dragon fruit, also known as pitaya, is an exotic pink-skinned fruit of the cactus family. Indigenous to Mexico, it has been transported around the world, and is particularly popular in South East Asia. In Australia the fruit is grown in the tropical north. The flesh can be either yellow, red or white, with a mild taste like kiwifruit, and with similar small textural black seeds.

PAPAYA POWER BOWL

PREP TIME 20 MINUTES (+ FREEZING) SERVES 2

You will need to start this recipe a day ahead.

- 2 pink dragon fruit (pitaya) (850g)
- 2 tablespoons raw honey
- ¼ cup (60ml) lime juice
- 1 small orange papaya, halved lengthways, seeded

- 1 small banana (130g), sliced
- 1 kiwifruit, halved crossways
- 2 purple figs, halved lengthways
- 125g (4 ounces) fresh or frozen raspberries
- cherries and lime wedges, to serve

1 Peel and coarsely chop dragon fruit. Transfer to a freezer-proof container. Freeze overnight or until firm.

2 Blend frozen dragon fruit with honey and lime juice until smooth.

3 Divide dragon fruit mixture between papaya halves or two wide bowls. Top with banana, kiwifruit, fig and raspberries. Serve with cherries and lime wedges.

HEALTH FACTS Fruit contains sugar in an unrefined form, along with beneficial fibre and antioxidants. Dragon fruit (pitaya) are a very low-kilojoule fruit, rich in vitamins C, B1, B2 and B3, plus, one small fruit is said to contain eight percent of our daily iron needs.

ZA'ATAR-ROASTED TOMATO, BACON AND EGG CUPS

- 6 cherry tomatoes (120g), halved
- 1½ tablespoons olive oil
- 1 teaspoon za'atar (see tip)
- 4 slices shortcut bacon rashers (140g), chopped finely
- 1 medium onion (150g), chopped finely

- 10 eggs
- ¼ cup finely chopped fresh flat-leaf parsley
- ¼ cup (60ml) pouring cream
- ¼ cup (60g) fresh ricotta, crumbled

1 Preheat oven to 180°C/350°F. Grease a 6-hole (¾ cup/180ml) texas muffin pan; line each hole with two 15cm (6-inch) squares of baking paper. Line a small oven tray with baking paper.

2 Place tomatoes on lined tray; drizzle with 2 teaspoons of the oil, sprinkle with za'atar. Bake for 20 minutes or until tender.

3 Meanwhile, heat remaining oil in a large frying pan over medium heat. Cook bacon and onion for 5 minutes or until soft and browned. Spoon into lined muffin holes. Whisk eggs, parsley and cream in a large bowl; season. Pour into muffin cases.

4 Bake cups for 20 minutes. Top with ricotta and tomatoes; bake egg cups for a further 5 minutes or until set. Season; serve warm or at room temperature.

SWAP OUT bacon and replace with tofu bacon (see page 92) to make the recipe vegetarian.

SERVE WITH a salad of radishes wedges, snow pea sprouts and halved sugar snap peas or pea pods, if you like.

TIP Za'atar is a Middle-Eastern spice blend that generally includes thyme, sesame seeds, sumac and cumin in equal proportions, with a little salt. You could also use dukkah or ½ teaspoon smoked paprika instead.

TIP If you don't
have a honey allergy,
serve with bee
pollen, if you like.
Alternatively, serve
with fennel pollen,
which are the flower
tips and pollen from
fennel flowers,
available from health
food or spice stores.

CHERRY, GINGER AND CHIA BIRCHER

PREP TIME **20 MINUTES (+ REFRIGERATION)** SERVES **4 (MAKES 5 CUPS)**

- 2 cups (300g) frozen pitted cherries
- 2 fresh dates, pitted
- 5cm (2-inch) piece fresh ginger, chopped coarsely
- 1¼ cups (310ml) water
- ½ cup (140g) unsweetened coconut yoghurt
- 1 cup (90g) rolled oats
- ½ cup (80g) white chia seeds
- ¼ cup (50g) pepitas (pumpkin seed kernels)
- 1 tablespoon pure maple syrup
- 1 small green apple (130g)
- ¼ cup (40g) natural almonds, roasted, chopped
- fresh cherries and bee pollen (see tip), to serve, optional

1 Process cherries, dates, ginger and the water until smooth. Pour into a large bowl.

2 Stir in coconut yoghurt, oats, chia seeds, pepitas and syrup until combined. Cover with plastic wrap; refrigerate for 2 hours or until thickened, or overnight.

3 Coarsely grate apple and stir through soaked bircher mixture. Divide bircher among four bowls, serve sprinkled with almonds. Top with fresh cherries and bee pollen, if you like.

MAKE & SAVE

COCONUT AND VANILLA ICE-CREAM SANDWICHES

PREP TIME 1 HOUR (+ STANDING & FREEZING) MAKES 15 SANDWICHES

You will need to start this recipe 2 days ahead.

- ⅔ cup (160ml) coconut cream
- 1 cup (150g) raw cashews
- 3 young drinking coconuts (3.6kg)
- ½ cup (125ml) rice malt syrup
- ¼ cup (60ml) coconut cream, extra
- 3 teaspoons pure vanilla extract
- 1 vanilla bean, split lengthways, seeds scraped
- 200g (7 ounces) dark (semi-sweet) vegan chocolate (see tip), chopped coarsely
- 1 tablespoon coconut oil, melted, extra

CHOCOLATE BISCUITS

- ¾ cup (120g) natural almonds
- ¾ cup (130g) activated buckwheat groats
- ⅔ cup (50g) desiccated coconut
- ½ cup (50g) cacao powder
- ⅓ cup (80ml) pure maple syrup
- ¼ cup (50g) coconut oil, melted
- ½ teaspoon pure vanilla extract

1 To make the coconut ice-cream, pour coconut cream into an ice-cube tray and freeze overnight.

2 Meanwhile, place cashews in a medium bowl; cover with cold water. Stand for 4 hours or overnight. Drain cashews, rinse under cold water; drain well.

3 Line an 18cm x 28cm (7¼-inch x 11¼-inch) slice pan with plastic wrap, extending the plastic 5cm (2 inches) over the sides.

4 Place a coconut on its side on a chopping board; carefully cut off the dome-shaped top with a cleaver or large knife — you will need to use a bit of force. Drain coconut water into a large jug. Spoon out the soft flesh. Repeat with remaining coconuts; you should have about 3 cups (270g) coconut flesh.

5 Blend coconut flesh with drained cashews, syrup, extra coconut cream, vanilla extract and seeds until as smooth as possible, using a high-powered blender if available; this type of blender will produce a very smooth consistency. Add coconut cream ice-cubes; blend until well combined. Pour into lined pan. Freeze overnight or until firm.

6 Make chocolate biscuits.

7 Remove ice-cream from pan. Cut into 15 rounds using a 5cm (2-inch) cutter. Place a round of ice-cream on half the biscuits, flatten slightly and sandwich with a second biscuit.

8 Place chocolate in a small heatproof bowl over a saucepan of gently simmering water (don't allow bowl to touch water); stir until just melted. Add extra coconut oil; stir to combine. Pour melted chocolate into a small deep bowl.

9 Dip ice-cream sandwiches into melted chocolate to half-coat. Allow excess chocolate to drain off, place on a tray lined with baking paper (or balance on egg rings, choc-dipped half facing up); freeze for 10 minutes or until chocolate is set.

CHOCOLATE BISCUITS

Process all ingredients until coarse crumbs form and mixture starts to come together. Roll between two sheets baking paper until 3mm (⅛-inch) thick. Place on oven tray. Freeze for 15 minutes or until firm. Cut into 30 rounds using a 5cm (2-inch) cutter, re-rolling scraps. Return biscuits to tray, cover with plastic wrap; freeze until needed.

TRY THIS You can set the ice-cream in a 3 cup (750ml) capacity freezer-proof container, then place scoops between the biscuits, if preferred.

KEEPS Ice-cream can be frozen for up to 2 months. You can assemble ice-cream sandwiches ahead of time and store in an airtight container in the freezer between sheets of baking paper.

TIP Vegan chocolate
is available from
health food stores.

TIP Yacon syrup is available from some health food stores. It has a consistency similar to rice malt syrup, with a distinct treacle-like flavour and a mild level of sweetness.

SESAME GINGER DIPPING SAUCE

PREP TIME **5 MINUTES** MAKES **1 CUP (250ML)**

- 70g (2½-ounce) piece fresh ginger, grated finely
- ¼ cup (70g) unhulled tahini
- 2 tablespoons sesame oil
- 2 tablespoons tamari

- 2 tablespoons apple cider vinegar
- 2 tablespoons yacon syrup (see tips) or coconut nectar
- ½ fresh long red chilli, seeded, sliced thinly, optional

1 Press grated ginger through a sieve over a small bowl; you need 2 tablespoons ginger juice. Discard pulp.

2 Combine ginger juice with tahini, sesame oil, tamari, vinegar and yacon syrup in a small bowl; stir until smooth. Add chilli, if you like.

TRY THIS as a dipping sauce for rice paper rolls or as a dressing on salads, rawslaws, kelp noodles and steamed vegetables.

KEEPS Store in a sealed glass jar in the fridge for up to 1 week.

✳ Traditionally, kefir is a fermented milk product of Russian origin made by using a culture of kefir grains, comprising of a number of different bacteria and yeasts. The yeasts ferment the sugar in milk to create carbon dioxide and alcohol. These kefir grains can be use with other liquids to create an effervescent mixture, however, for this to work some sugar needs to be present, which is then mostly converted to carbon dioxide, producing a refreshing healthy, sparkling drink.

WATER KEFIR SODA

PREP TIME **30 MINUTES (+ FERMENTATION)** MAKES **1 LITRE**

You will need to start this recipe at least 4 days ahead.

- 2 tablespoons raw sugar
- ¼ cup (60ml) boiling water
- 1 litre (4 cups) bottled filtered water
- 1 tablespoon hydrated water kefir grains (see tips)
- 1 slice lemon
- 1 dried apricot or fig

1 Sterilise a 1.25 litre (5 cup) glass jar. For details on 'how to sterilise' see page 236.
2 Place sugar and the boiling water in sterilised jar; stir until sugar dissolves. Add the filtered water. Check the mixture is now at room temperature; if not, leave to cool further.
3 Add kefir grains, lemon slice and dried fruit; cover top of jar with muslin and secure with an elastic band or kitchen string (this allows kefir to breathe and prevents contamination). Leave jar on a work bench at a stable room temperature for at least 72 hours (see tips).
4 After first ferment, strain liquid into a sterilised 1 litre (4-cup) glass jar or bottle with a tight-fitting lid; add one of the suggested flavour combinations opposite. Seal; leave jar on a work bench at a stable room temperature to ferment for a further 12-24 hours.
5 Refrigerate after second ferment to slow down fermentation process. Strain flavourings before serving. Certain flavour combinations will fizz more than others, so open carefully when ready to drink.

FLAVOUR COMBINATIONS

BEETROOT
Add 2 thin slices fresh beetroot, cut into julienne, to the strained kefir liquid before second fermenting.

GREEN APPLE & SPIRULINA
Add 3 thin slices green apple and ⅛ teaspoon spirulina to the strained kefir liquid before second fermenting.

FRESH TURMERIC & GINGER
Peel and slice a 3cm (1¼-inch) piece fresh tturmeric and a 3cm (1¼-inch) piece ginger; add to the strained kefir liquid before second fermenting.

RASPBERRY
Add 8 fresh raspberries to the strained kefir liquid before second fermenting.

PINEAPPLE & PASSIONFRUIT
Add one 2cm x 5cm (¾-inch x 2-inch) piece of peeled pineapple and the pulp of 1 passionfruit to the strained kefir liquid before second fermenting.

KEEPS Store water kefir soda in the fridge for up to 2 weeks.

GREEN APPLE
& SPIRULINA

Beetroot

Fresh turmeric
& ginger

Raspberry

PINEAPPLE
& PASSIONFRUIT

TIPS Water kefir grains are available from health food stores or are readily available to purchase online. Freeze leftover grains for up to 12 months. In warmer months kefir will ferment faster. Taste it after 24 hours; it should taste slightly sour. The longer it is left, the more the sugar will be converted to carbon dioxide, and the more sour the taste will be.

✳ Biscuits have a reputation for being fat and sugar traps but not these guys! While they do of course contain some fat, the fat in nuts is considered to be a 'good fat'. Add to that the protein power of chickpeas and chia seeds and you have a great pick-me-up cookie for mid-morning lulls, 3pm slumps, or post-work out.

PB AND J CHICKPEA COOKIES

PREP + COOK TIME 1 HOUR (+ STANDING) MAKES 18

- 400g (12½ ounces) canned chickpeas, drained, rinsed
- ½ cup (135g) crunchy natural peanut butter
- ¼ cup (60ml) pure maple syrup
- 1 teaspoon pure vanilla extract
- 1 teaspoon baking powder
- ½ teaspoon sea salt

RASPBERRY CHIA JAM
- ½ cup (75g) frozen raspberries, thawed
- 1 tablespoon water
- 1 tablespoon white chia seeds
- 2 teaspoons pure maple syrup

1 Make raspberry chia jam.

2 Preheat oven to 180°C/350°F. Line a large oven tray with baking paper.

3 Pat chickpeas dry with paper towel. Process chickpeas, peanut butter, syrup, vanilla, baking powder and salt, scraping down side of the food processor bowl several times, until smooth.

4 Using damp hands, roll tablespoonfuls of mixture into balls, place on tray; flatten with the palm of your hand into a 4cm (1½-inch) round. Spoon 1 teaspoon raspberry chia jam onto centre of each cookie.

5 Bake cookies for 15 minutes or until golden and a cookie can be gently pushed without breaking. Cool on tray.

RASPBERRY CHIA JAM
Blend or process raspberries and the water until pureed. Transfer to a bowl; stir in chia seeds and syrup. Cover with plastic wrap; refrigerate for at least 1 hour until thickened to a jam-like consistency.

KEEPS Store cookies in an airtight container in the fridge for up to 1 week.

GOLDEN AND RED SAUERKRAUTS

PREP TIME **45 MINUTES (+ FERMENTATION)**

GOLDEN SAUERKRAUT

- 1 small white cabbage (1.2kg)
- 3 medium carrots (360g), peeled
- 2 cloves garlic, crushed
- 5cm (2-inch) piece ginger, grated finely
- 5cm (2-inch) piece turmeric, grated finely
- 2 teaspoons caraway seeds
- 2 teaspoons fennel seeds
- 1 tablespoon sea salt

RED SAUERKRAUT

- 1 small red cabbage (1.2kg)
- 2 medium beetroot (350g), peeled
- 2 cloves garlic, crushed
- 2 teaspoons cumin seeds
- 2 teaspoons juniper berries
- 1 tablespoon sea salt

1 Sterilise two 1.5 litre (6-cup) jars. For details on 'how to sterilise' see page 236.

2 For both golden and red sauerkraut, wash exterior of each cabbage, carrot and beetroot well. Pull off two outer layers from each cabbage and reserve.

3 Using a food processor fitted with a fine slicing attachment, slice white cabbage. Change the attachment to a coarse grater; grate carrot. Transfer to a large bowl. Wash food processor bowl; using the fine slicing attachment, slice red cabbage. Using the coarse grater attachment, grate beetroot. Transfer red vegetables to a second large bowl. (If you don't have a food processor with attachments, thinly slice the cabbage with a sharp cook's knife and grate the carrot and beetroot coarsely using a box grater.)

4 Add remaining golden sauerkraut ingredients to the first bowl and remaining red sauerkraut ingredients to the second bowl. Wearing plastic gloves, massage vegetables in each bowl for 15 minutes or until they release their moisture and soften. (Wash gloves in between mixing to avoid transferring flavours and colours between each bowl.)

5 Spoon each sauerkraut mixture tightly into a sterilised jar, pressing it down firmly to remove air pockets and to ensure that the top layer is covered by cabbage juice. Fold reserved white cabbage leaves in half; place over golden sauerkraut. Repeat with reserved red cabbage leaves for red sauerkraut. Make sure there is about a 1cm (½-inch) gap at the top of the jars for juices to gather. Seal jars.

6 Leave jars to ferment at room temperature for 3-4 weeks (see tips). When sauerkraut is ready it will have an acidic taste and a soft but not mushy texture. Discard the folded cabbage leaf; store sauerkraut in the fridge to halt the fermentation process.

TRY THIS

In rainbow salads for a piquant addition.

Layer between bread with corned beef and swiss cheese, then toast for reuben sandwiches.

Stir a little sour cream and chopped fresh dill through sauerkraut and serve with smoked cured fish.

KEEPS Once fermented, store in the fridge for up to 3 months.

TIPS The time for fermentation to occur depends on the time of year. In warmer months it will be approximately three weeks, while in cooler months expect to wait up to four weeks; it's normal for the mixture to bubble and fizz a bit.

TIP Peaches, nectarines, apricots and even plums are all suitable fruit for making this jam.

✳ This is not a proper jam, but that's a good thing, since it means it's fast, foolproof and has a fraction of the sugar. Rather than relying on the interaction between pectin and sugar to create a gel, the natural thickening qualities of chia seed provide a jam-like quality.

INSTANT STONEFRUIT AND PASSIONFRUIT CHIA JAM

PREP TIME **5 MINUTES (+ STANDING)** MAKES **1½ CUPS**

- 2 tablespoons white chia seeds
- ¼ cup (60ml) water
- 2 ripe peaches or nectarines (300g), chopped coarsely (see tip)

- 2 tablespoons raw honey
- ½ vanilla bean, split lengthways, seeds scraped
- 1 passionfruit, halved, pulp removed

1 Place chia seeds in a small bowl, stir in the water; stand for 5 minutes.
2 Place fruit in a bowl; crush with the back of a fork. Add chia seed mixture and remaining ingredients; stir until combined.

TRY THIS
Spooned over thick sugar-free coconut or Greek-style yoghurt, with sliced nectarine or peach.
Swirled through a multi-grain porridge.
Spread over ricotta on grainy bread.

<u>KEEPS</u> Store jam in an airtight container in the fridge for up to 1 week or freezer for up to 1 month.

DANDELION STICKY CHAI MIX

PREP + COOK TIME **15 MINUTES** MAKES **1⅓ CUPS**

- 2 tablespoons cardamom pods
- 4 cinnamon sticks, broken into pieces
- 8 star anise
- 2 teaspoons fennels seeds
- ⅔ cup (70g) roasted dandelion (see tip)
- 2 tablespoons finely grated fresh ginger
- 2 teaspoons ground turmeric
- 1 teaspoon vanilla bean paste
- ⅓ cup (115g) honey
- 2 tablespoons lemon juice

1 Heat a small frying pan over medium heat. Add cardamom, cinnamon, star anise and fennel seeds; cook, stirring continuously for 2 minutes or until lightly toasted. Grind using a mortar and pestle until crushed finely.

2 Place roasted dandelion in a small bowl; stir through toasted spices, ginger, turmeric and vanilla.

3 Place honey in a small heatproof cup; sit cup in a small bowl of boiling water, stir until thin and runny. Stir honey and lemon juice through dandelion mixture. Transfer chai mix to a small screw-top jar; seal and refrigerate.

TIP Roasted dandelion is made from the roasted roots and leaves of the dandelion plant. It is available from some supermarkets, health food stores and online.

TRY THIS Make a delicious dandy chai for two. Place 1 teaspoon of chai mix and 1 cup water in a small saucepan. Bring to the boil; remove from heat. Add 1 cup of your favourite milk, return pan to medium heat; cook, stirring, until mixture boils. Immediately remove from heat; steep for 3 minutes. Pour into your favourite cups or mugs; serve sprinkled with ground cinnamon.

KEEPS Store in the fridge for up to 1 month.

BASIC BROTHS

Hot broth is a great healthy alternative to tea or coffee.
Broths can be made up to 3 days ahead; keep, covered,
in the refrigerator, or freeze for up to 3 months.

SLOW-COOKER BEEF BONE BROTH

PREP + COOK TIME
17 HOURS (+ COOLING
& REFRIGERATION)
MAKES 2 LITRES (8 CUPS)

Preheat oven to 220°C/450°F. Place 1kg (2lbs) beef bones (cut into short lengths by your butcher) in a roasting pan; roast for 30 minutes or until golden. Transfer to a 5 litre (20-cup) slow cooker set on lowest setting. Add 1 quartered medium brown onion, 2 coarsely chopped, trimmed celery stalks, 3 sprigs fresh thyme, 2 teaspoons black peppercorns and 3.5 litres (14 cups) filtered water; it should fill to 1cm (½-inch) from top. Add 1 tablespoon apple cider vinegar; cook, covered, for 16 hours. Strain stock through a muslin-lined sieve into a heatproof bowl; discard solids. Cool. Cover; refrigerate for 12 hours.

TIP Broth may turn to jelly; this is due to the gelatine from bones. Skim and discard surface fat before using, or refrigerate fat for up to 3 days and use instead of oil when roasting vegetables.

VEGETABLE BROTH

PREP + COOK TIME
2¼ HOURS (+ COOLING
& REFRIGERATION)
MAKES 3 LITRES (12 CUPS)

Place 4 coarsely chopped onions, 2 coarsely chopped large carrots, 8 coarsely chopped trimmed celery stalks, 2 coarsely chopped large parsnips, 8 peeled cloves garlic, 6 stalks fresh flat-leaf parsley, 2 teaspoons black peppercorns and 4 litres (16 cups) water in a large heavy-based saucepan; bring to the boil. Reduce heat to low; simmer for 1½ hours. Add 200g (6½oz) coarsely chopped cup mushrooms and 4 coarsely chopped tomatoes; simmer for a further 30 minutes. Strain stock through a muslin-lined sieve into a heatproof bowl; discard solids. Season with sea salt. Cool. Cover; refrigerate until cold.

FISH BROTH

PREP + COOK TIME
45 MINUTES (+ COOLING
& REFRIGERATION)
MAKES 2 LITRES (8 CUPS)

Place 1.5kg (3lbs) fish bones, 3 litres (12 cups) water, 1 coarsely chopped brown onion, 2 coarsely chopped trimmed celery stalks, 6 stalks fresh flat-leaf parsley and 1 teaspoon black peppercorns in a large heavy-based saucepan; bring to the boil. Reduce heat to low; simmer for 30 minutes. Strain stock through a muslin-lined sieve into a heatproof bowl; discard solids. Season with sea salt and 2 tablespoons lemon juice. Cool. Cover; refrigerate until cold. Skim and discard any surface fat before using.

CHICKEN BROTH

PREP + COOK TIME
6¼ HOURS (+ COOLING
& REFRIGERATION)
MAKES 3 LITRES (12 CUPS)

Place 2kg (4lbs) chicken bones, 2 tablespoons apple cider vinegar, 2 coarsely chopped medium brown onions, 2 coarsely chopped trimmed celery stalks, 2 coarsely chopped medium carrots, 8 peeled cloves garlic, 6 stalks fresh flat-leaf parsley, 2 teaspoons black peppercorns and 5 litres (20 cups) water in a large heavy-based saucepan; bring to the boil. Reduce heat to low; simmer for 6 hours, skimming the surface occasionally. Strain stock through a muslin-lined sieve into a heatproof bowl; discard solids. Season with sea salt. Cool. Cover; refrigerate until cold. Skim and discard surface fat before using.

PINEAPPLE GINGER BEER

PREP TIME **10 MINUTES (+ STANDING)** MAKES **2 LITRES (8 CUPS)**

You will need a 25cm (10-inch) piece muslin and to start this recipe 2 days ahead.

- 1 medium pineapple (1.25kg)
- 150g (4½ ounces) fresh ginger, peeled, chopped coarsely
- ½ cup (75g) raisins
- 1 cup (240g) rice malt syrup
- ¼ cup (60ml) lemon juice
- 1.75 litres (7 cups) water
- ¼ teaspoon dried yeast

1 Peel and coarsely chop pineapple, including core.

2 Process pineapple and ginger until chopped finely. Combine with remaining ingredients in a large stainless steel or glass bowl. Cover bowl with muslin; secure with kitchen string. Set aside at room temperature for 36 hours or until mixture is fizzy.

3 Strain into airtight sterilised bottles (see page 236) and refrigerate.

KEEPS Store the ginger beer in the fridge for up to 2 months. Take care when opening, as it will fizz up.

TIPS You could use a
clean plastic bucket
to brew the ginger
beer if you don't
have a large enough
bowl. The number of
days it takes to
become fizzy will vary
slightly, depending
on room temperature.

ROSEMARY AND CACAO CRACKERS

PREP + COOK TIME **40 MINUTES** MAKES **25**

- 1½ cups (180g) almond meal
- 2 tablespoons cacao powder
- 1 teaspoon finely chopped fresh rosemary
- 1 teaspoon sea salt flakes
- 1 tablespoon extra virgin olive oil
- 1 egg
- 1 teaspoon extra virgin olive oil, extra
- 1 tablespoon fresh rosemary leaves, extra

1 Preheat oven to 180°C/360°F.
2 Combine almond meal, sifted cacao, rosemary and ½ teaspoon salt in a large bowl. Whisk oil and egg together in a small bowl, add to cacao mixture; using clean hands, combine well to form a dough.
3 Shape dough into a ball; place between two sheets of baking paper. Roll out to a 2mm (⅛-inch) thick, 20cm x 30cm (8-inch x 12-inch) rectangle. Transfer dough on paper to a large oven tray; remove top sheet of baking paper.
4 Using a sharp knife, trim the edges of the dough straight; cut into five lengthways and crossways to make 25 pieces, 4cm x 6cm (1½-inch x 2½-inch) in size. Brush with extra olive oil. Sprinkle with extra rosemary and remaining salt.
5 Bake crackers, rotating tray halfway through cooking, for 20 minutes or until golden. Cool on tray.

TRY WITH a sugar-free dip or your favourite cheese, such as parmesan, double brie or vintage cheddar.

KEEPS Store crackers in an airtight container for up to 5 days.

* We've created this recipe with vegans and the
  dairy intolerant in mind. The cheese spread is
  multi-purpose, see 'try this' for suggested uses.

SMOKED 'CHEESE' SPREAD

PREP TIME **10 MINUTES (+ STANDING)** MAKES **1½ CUPS**

You will need to start this recipe a day ahead.

- ½ cup (75g) raw cashews
- ½ cup (70g) raw macadamias
- 1 tablespoon lemon juice
- 2 tablespoons nutritional yeast
  flakes (see page 236)
- 1½ teaspoons apple cider vinegar
- 1½ teaspoons smoked paprika
- 1 teaspoon ground turmeric
- ¼ teaspoon onion powder
- ½ teaspoon garlic powder
- ½ cup (125ml) almond and
  cashew milk
- 1 teaspoon white (shiro) miso

1 Place cashews and macadamias in two separate small bowls; cover with cold water. Stand, covered, for 4 hours or overnight. Drain nuts, rinse under cold water; drain well.

2 Blend drained nuts with remaining ingredients, using a high-powered blender if available; this type of blender will produce a very smooth consistency.

<u>TRY THIS</u> spooned over oven-baked tortillas; serve topped with sugar-free dill pickles, pickled jalapeños, lime wedges and coriander (cilantro).

<u>KEEPS</u> Store in an airtight container in the fridge for up to 3 weeks.

NO-NASTIES CHILLI SAUCE

PREP + COOK TIME **40 MINUTES (+ STANDING)** MAKES **3 CUPS**

- 4 bulbs garlic, cloves separated, unpeeled
- 400g (13 ounces) fresh long red chillies, half seeded, all chopped coarsely (see notes above)
- 2 cups (500ml) rice wine vinegar
- ¼ cup (90g) honey
- 2 tablespoons sea salt flakes
- 2 teaspoons cornflour (cornstarch)
- 1 tablespoon tamari

1 Place garlic in a medium saucepan, cover with cold water, bring to the boil; simmer for 1 minute. Scoop garlic from water with a slotted spoon. Rinse under cold water, drain; peel skins. Return to boiling water for 30 seconds; drain again. (Cooking the first time will assist with peeling, blanching the second time helps mellow the garlic flavour.)
2 Combine garlic, chilli and vinegar in same medium saucepan. Bring to the boil; boil for 4 minutes or until chilli is just tender. Remove from heat; stand 10 minutes to cool slightly.
3 Blend or process chilli mixture, honey, sea salt and cornflour until smooth.
4 Strain chilli mixture through a fine sieve back into same saucepan; discard solids. Bring chilli mixture to the boil. Reduce heat to medium; simmer, stirring occasionally, for 10 minutes or until thickened slightly and to allow flavours to develop. Stir in tamari; cool.

TRY THIS
Spooned over corn chips, guacamole, grilled corn kernels amd mixed halved cherry tomatoes for a healthy 'nachos', sprinkled with coriander sprigs, with lime wedges to the side.
Drizzled over sweet potato hash to complement the sweetness of the potatoes.
Brushed over uncooked prawns with a mix of crushed garlic and lemon grass before grilling.
Stirred through fried brown rice or other rice dishes.

KEEPS Store in an airtight jar in the fridge for up to 4 months.

LOADS-IN-ONE GOODNESS SMASH

PREP + COOK TIME 25 MINUTES (+ STANDING) MAKES 2 CUPS

This versatile smash can be used to power-up loads of meals and snacks.

- 500g (1 pound) frozen broad (fava) beans
- 1 clove garlic, crushed
- 1 medium avocado (250g), sliced
- 2 tablespoons lemon juice
- 1 nori (seaweed) sheet, crumbled coarsely
- 1 tablespoon sesame seeds, toasted
- ½ teaspoon sesame oil

1 Place beans in a large bowl with enough boiling water to cover; stand for 1 minute. Drain; cool under cold running water. Peel skins. Pulse peeled beans just until chopped coarsely.

2 Transfer beans to a medium bowl. Add remaining ingredients; stir to combine. Mash lightly with a fork until avocado is mashed coarsely; season to taste.

<u>TRY THIS</u>

Spooned over roasted sweet potato wedges, sprinkled with small mint leaves and served with lime wedges.

Dolloped over cooked eggs for breakfast.

Stirred through warm or cold soba or green tea noodles.

Spread over rosemary and cacao crackers (see page 65).

With a little extra chopped fresh mint and lemon juice stirred in, if you're in the mood for a little more zing.

<u>KEEPS</u> Cover surface with plastic wrap and store in an airtight container in the fridge for up to 2 days.

SEED, DATE AND TAHINI SPREAD

PREP TIME **10 MINUTES (+ STANDING)** MAKES **1 CUP**

- 1 cup (230g) fresh dates, pitted
- ⅓ cup (90g) hulled tahini
- 2 teaspoons sesame seeds
- 2 teaspoons linseeds (flaxseeds)
- 1 teaspoon poppy seeds
- ⅛ teaspoon sea salt flakes

1 Place dates in a small heatproof bowl, cover with boiling water; stand 5 minutes. Drain; reserve 2 tablespoons liquid. Blend or process dates with reserved liquid, tahini, seeds and salt until smooth.

2 Spoon seed, date and tahini butter into a jar and refrigerate.

VARIATION For a chocolate spread, blend in 1 tablespoon cacao powder with all the ingredients.

TRY THIS
Folded through coconut or Greek-style yoghurt for a natural sweet treat.
Spread over pancakes or toast in place of jam.
Stirred into a banana smoothie.
Blended with ricotta as a topping for cakes.

KEEPS Store spread in an airtight jar in the fridge for up to 6 weeks.

CHEESY PARSNIP TEFF BREAD

PREP + COOK TIME **1 HOUR 20 MINUTES (+ STANDING)** SERVES **6**

- 3 cups (375g) grated parsnip
- 1½ cups (240g) ivory teff flour (see tips)
- 1½ cups (180g) grated vintage cheddar
- 1½ teaspoons baking powder
- 3 eggs
- ¾ cup (180ml) milk
- ⅓ cup (80ml) olive oil

1 Preheat oven to 180°C/350°F. Grease a 7cm x 25cm (2¾-inch x 10-inch) loaf pan or 1.25 litre (5 cup) terrine mould. Line base and long sides with baking paper, extending the paper 5cm (2 inches) over long sides.

2 Combine parsnip, teff, cheddar and baking powder in a large bowl. Season. Whisk eggs, milk and oil in a small bowl; stir through parsnip mixture. Spoon into tin; smooth top.

3 Bake for 1 hour 10 minutes or until a skewer inserted into the centre comes out clean; cover loosely with foil half way through cooking if it starts to overbrown. Stand loaf in pan for 15 minutes before turning, top-side up, onto a wire rack to cool completely. Slice and toast to serve.

TRY THIS with different toppings, such as boiled eggs seasoned with salt and pepper, sprinkled with parsely sprigs. For more ideas, see page 77.

KEEPS Store bread, wrapped in plastic wrap in an airtight container, for up to 3 days.

TIPS Teff flour is derived from the seeds of a hardy grass. It is available from some supermarkets, delis and health food stores. You can use a loaf pan that is slightly longer and narrower, or wider and shorter, as long as the capacity of the pan is close to 5 cups. To check your pan, fill a jug with 5-cups water and pour into the pan.

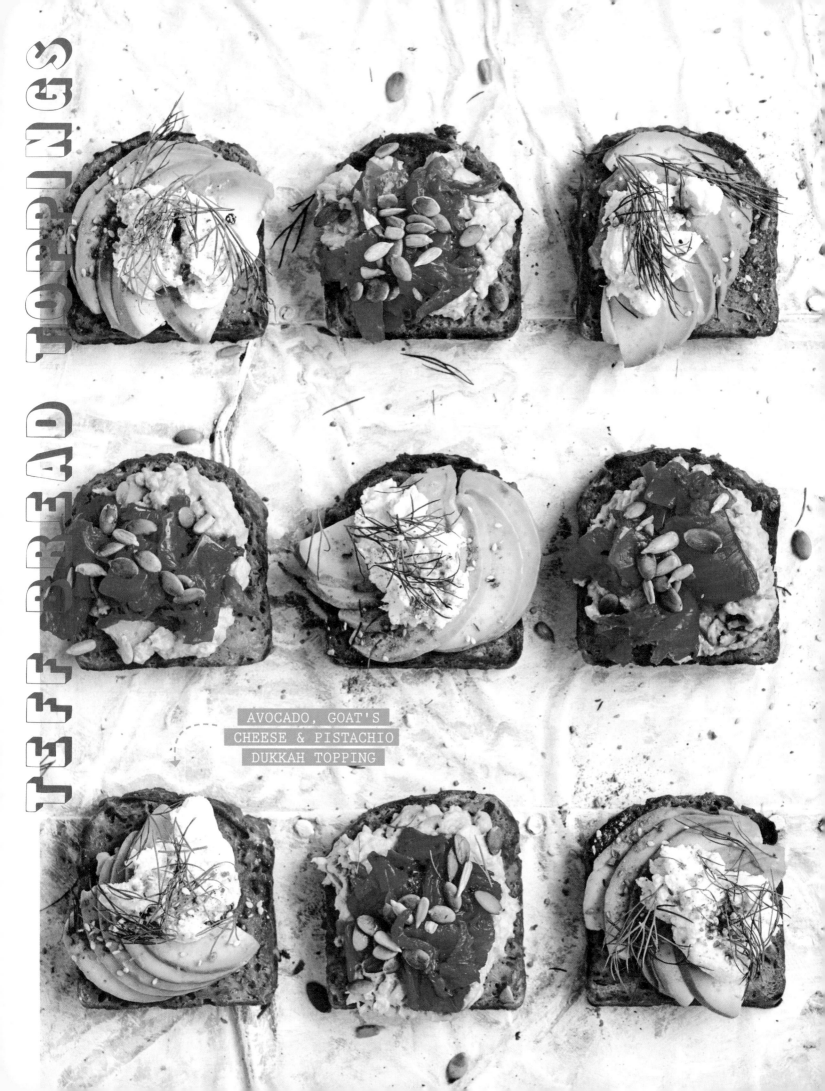

AVOCADO, GOAT'S CHEESE & PISTACHIO DUKKAH TOPPING

*Smashed avocado,
kimchi & seeds topping*

AVOCADO, GOAT'S CHEESE & PISTACHIO DUKKAH
PREP + COOKING TIME **5 MINUTES** SERVES **2**

Top toasted sliced teff bread (see page 74) with a quarter of a sliced avocado, 2 tablespoons marinated goat's cheese, a sprinkle of pistachio dukkah and a few dill sprigs.

SMASHED AVOCADO, KIMCHI & SEEDS
PREP + COOKING TIME **5 MINUTES** SERVES **2**

Mash a quarter of an avocado in a small bowl; season to taste. Spread on a slice of toasted teff bread (see page 74), then top with your favourite kimchi and a few pepitas (pumpkin seed kernels) amd sunflower seeds.

TIP We used Green St Kitchen's black miso and garlic kimchi.

✳ This amazing mayo is a bit of a game-changer for vegans or those allergic to eggs who have struggled to find a decent mayo comparable in taste to egg mayonnaise.

VEGAN MAYONNAISE

PREP TIME **5 MINUTES** MAKES **1 CUP**

- ¼ cup (60ml) aquafaba (liquid from canned chickpeas, see tip)
- 1 tablespoon apple cider vinegar
- ½ teaspoon sea salt flakes
- ½ teaspoon dijon mustard
- 1 cup (250ml) sunflower oil

1 Blend aquafaba, vinegar, salt and mustard in a small blender (do not use a food processor) until smooth. With the motor operating, add oil in a slow, steady stream until thick and creamy.

2 Spoon vegan mayonnaise into a jar and refrigerate.

VARIATIONS

LEMON AÏOLI

Substitute lemon juice for vinegar and stir in 1 crushed clove garlic and 1 teaspoon finely grated lemon rind at the end.

CHIPOTLE

Stir in 1 teaspoon Tabasco chipotle hot sauce (or to taste) and 1 teaspoon ground cumin at the end.

GREEN GENIUS

Blend in ¼ cup blanched chopped spinach leaves and 2 tablespoons coarsely chopped fresh dill.

KEEPS Store mayonnaise in an airtight container in the fridge for up to 1 month.

TIP Aquafaba (bean water) is the drained liquid from canned legumes; we prefer to use chickpeas (garbanzo beans). A 420g (13½-ounce) can will generally provide ½ cup (125ml) aquafaba. Leftover aquafaba will keep refrigerated for up to 2 days.

SALTED CARAMEL SAUCE

PREP + COOK TIME **15 MINUTES** MAKES **1 CUP**

- 160g (5 ounces) fresh dates, pitted,
  chopped coarsely
- 270ml (8½ ounces) coconut cream
- ½ vanilla bean, split lengthways,
  seeds scraped
- ¾ teaspoon fine sea salt

1 Blend all ingredients using a high-powered blender if available;
this type of blender will produce a very smooth consistency.
2 Transfer mixture to a small saucepan. Cook, stirring continuously
over low heat, for 10 minutes or until thickened.

<u>TIP</u> You can add 2 teaspoons cacao powder to the sauce for a hint of chocolate,
if you like.

<u>TRY THIS</u>
Drizzled over coconut and vanilla ice-cream (see page 46), scooped into
halved coconuts, topped with flaked coconut.
Dolloped over a stack of feather-light pancakes.
Swirled through frozen sugar-free yoghurt.
Thinned with a little water to drizzle.
Straight from the jar!

<u>KEEPS</u> Store salted caramel sauce in an airtight container in the fridge
for up to 1 week.

LUNCH OR DINNER

BEETROOT AND BUCKWHEAT RISOTTO WITH GOAT'S CURD

PREP + COOK TIME **2 HOURS** SERVES **6**

- 4 large beetroot (beets) (1.2kg), trimmed, leaves reserved
- ⅓ cup (80ml) extra virgin olive oil
- 2 tablespoons finely chopped fresh thyme
- ¾ cup (180ml) boiling water
- 1 teaspoon red wine vinegar
- 1 medium onion (150g), chopped finely
- 4 cloves garlic, chopped finely
- 1 bulb baby fennel (130g), trimmed, chopped finely
- 2 cups (400g) buckwheat
- ½ cup (125ml) dry white wine
- 1.25 litres (5 cups) vegetable stock, warmed
- ½ cup (40g) finely grated parmesan
- 40g (1½ ounces) butter
- 125g (4 ounces) goat's curd

1 Preheat oven to 200°C/400°F.
2 Place each beetroot on a square of foil; drizzle with 1 tablespoon of the oil, season and sprinkle with 1 tablespoon of the thyme. Wrap tightly to enclose; place on an oven tray. Bake for 1¼ hours or until tender. When cool enough to handle, remove skin from beetroot.
3 Blend 3 of the beetroot in a high-powered blender (or a food processor) with the boiling water until smooth. Cut remaining beetroot into thin wedges. Transfer to a small bowl, toss with 1 tablespoon of the olive oil and vinegar; season to taste.
4 Heat remaining 2 tablespoons of the olive oil in a large, deep cast iron or other heavy-based saucepan over medium heat. Add onion, garlic, fennel and remaining thyme; cook for 5 minutes or until onion softens. Add buckwheat; cook, stirring, for 1 minute or until coated. Add wine; cook, stirring, for 1 minute.

5 Add stock and beetroot puree; bring to the boil. Reduce heat to low; simmer for 25 minutes, stirring occasionally or until buckwheat is tender. Stir in parmesan and butter. Season to taste, cover; stand for 2 minutes.
6 Serve risotto topped with goat's curd, beetroot wedges and reserved beetroot leaves.

SWAP OUT Barley can be substituted for buckwheat.

TIPS Choose a bunch
of beetroot with
beautiful small
leaves, as they are
also used in the
recipe. Goat's curd
is available from
large supermarkets
and delis; stir in a
bowl before using for
a smoother texture.
You could also top
the risotto with
crumbled fresh goat's
cheese or ricotta,
(see page 28).

TIPS To balance out flavours, a little sweetener is required; add the unrefined sweetener of your choice. Spiralisers are available from kitchen and homeware stores. Alternatively, you can cut the zucchini into julienne (matchsticks), using a mandoline or sharp knife.

✳ Use our beef bone broth recipe on page 61 as
the base for this aromatic Vietnamese soup or, if
preferred, use a good-quality purchased broth or stock.

ZUCCHINI NOODLE
BEEF PHO

PREP + COOK TIME **35 MINUTES** SERVES **4**

- 1 litre (4 cups) beef bone broth (see page 61)
- 2 cups (500ml) water
- 5cm (2-inch) piece fresh ginger, sliced thinly
- 2 cloves garlic, sliced thinly
- 1 star anise
- 2 cinnamon sticks, broken
- 2 tablespoons fish sauce
- ½ teaspoon unrefined sugar (see tips)
- 4 small zucchini (360g), spiralised into noodles (see tips)

- 400g (12½-ounce) piece beef fillet, sliced thinly
- 1 fresh long red chilli, sliced thinly
- 1 cup (80g) bean sprouts
- 1 cup fresh thai basil leaves
- 1 cup fresh mint leaves
- 1 cup fresh coriander (cilantro) leaves
- 4 green onions (scallions), sliced thinly

1 Place broth, the water, ginger, garlic, spices, fish sauce and sugar in a large saucepan; bring to the boil. Reduce heat to low-medium; simmer for 20 minutes. Strain through a fine sieve into a large heatproof bowl; discard solids.
2 Divide zucchini noodles among bowls; top with raw sliced beef and ladle over hot stock. Serve topped with chilli, bean sprouts, herbs and green onion.

Poke, pronounced POH-key, is a traditional Hawaiian
dish of marinated raw fish and rice. As with any raw
fish dish, it's important that the seafood is impeccably
fresh. We served this in hollowed out halved coconuts.

HAWAIIAN POKE WITH BROWN RICE

PREP + COOK TIME **35 MINUTES** SERVES **4**

- 1 cup (200g) brown rice
- 3 cups (750ml) water
- 2 teaspoons each white and black sesame seeds
- ⅓ cup (80ml) soy sauce
- 2 teaspoons rice wine vinegar
- 2 teaspoons sesame oil
- 500g (1 pound) sushi-grade tuna, cut into 1.5cm (¾-inch) cubes

- 2 green onions (scallions), sliced thinly
- 1 medium (250g) avocado, diced
- 250g (8 ounces) seaweed salad (see tip)
- 1 lebanese cucumber (130g), sliced

1 Place rice in a sieve; rinse under cold running water until water runs clear. Place rice and the water in a medium saucepan; bring to the boil over medium-high heat. Reduce heat to low; cook, covered, for 25 minutes or until rice is tender and water is absorbed.

2 Meanwhile, place a small frying pan over medium heat; cook sesame seeds, stirring continuously for 2 minutes or until golden.

3 Whisk soy sauce, vinegar, sesame oil and three-quarters of the sesame seeds in a medium jug. Toss tuna and three-quarters of the green onion with half of the soy dressing, cover with plastic wrap; marinate in the fridge for at least 5 minutes.

4 Divide brown rice evenly among bowls. Stir avocado gently into tuna mixture. Top rice with tuna mixture, seaweed salad and cucumber. Serve drizzled with remaining dressing, sprinkled with remaining sesame seeds and green onion.

TIP Seaweed salad is available from fishmongers, sushi bars and salad bars.

QUINOA AND BROWN RICE CHICKEN CONGEE

PREP + COOK TIME **2 HOURS 25 MINUTES** SERVES **6 (MAKES 10 CUPS)**

- 1 cup (200g) medium-grain brown rice, rinsed
- 2.5 litres (10 cups) water
- ¼ cup (50g) black or tri-coloured quinoa, rinsed
- 1 litre (4 cups) chicken stock
- 2 green onions (scallions), sliced thinly on the diagonal
- 2 cloves garlic, chopped finely
- 1 tablespoon finely grated ginger
- ½ teaspoon ground white pepper
- 1 tablespoon sesame oil
- 300g (9½ ounces) chicken breast fillet
- ¼ cup (40g) roasted almonds, chopped coarsely
- ¼ cup fresh coriander (cilantro) sprigs
- 2 tablespoons tamari
- extra sesame oil, to serve

1 Place rice and the water in a large saucepan; cover with a lid and bring to the boil. Reduce heat to medium; simmer, covered, for 1 hour. Add quinoa, stock, white part of green onion, garlic, ginger, white pepper, sesame oil and salt to taste. Cook, covered, for 30 minutes, stirring occasionally.

2 Add chicken to congee; cook, covered, for 12 minutes or until cooked through. Remove chicken with a slotted spoon; rest, loosely covered with foil, for 10 minutes. Shred chicken into bite-sized pieces.

3 Meanwhile, cook congee, uncovered, stirring occasionally, for a further 30 minutes or until rice has broken down and mixture is a soupy consistency. Add a little boiling water for a thinner consistency, if you like.

4 Ladle congee among bowls, top with remaining green onion, almonds and coriander sprigs. Serve drizzled with tamari and extra sesame oil.

✳ We've flipped the classic bacon, lettuce and tomato combo on its head, ditching the animal protein in favour of vegan-friendly tofu, which we've transformed with umami-rich flavours, so it's every bit as good bacon.

TOFU BACON BLAT

PREP + COOK TIME **40 MINUTES (+ REFRIGERATION)** SERVES **4**

You will need to start this recipe a day ahead.

- 8 large slices seeded sourdough rye bread (680g), toasted
- 1 large avocado (320g), mashed coarsely
- ½ cup (150g) purchased or homemade vegan mayonnaise (see page 78)
- 2 medium heirloom tomatoes (300g), sliced
- 8 butter lettuce leaves

TOFU BACON

- 375g (12 ounces) extra-firm tofu
- 1 tablespoon white (shiro) miso
- 1 tablespoon pure maple syrup
- 1 tablespoon tamari
- 1 teaspoon smoked paprika
- 1 tablespoon coconut oil, melted

1 Make tofu bacon.

2 Preheat oven to 220°C/425°F.

3 Bake one tray of the tofu bacon for 20 minutes, turning tofu over halfway through cooking, or until crisp and golden. Reserve remaining tofu bacon (see tips).

4 Spread half the toast evenly with avocado and mayonnaise. Top with tofu bacon, tomato and lettuce; season to taste. Sandwich with remaining toast.

TOFU BACON

Place tofu on a small wire rack over a deep-sided oven tray; cover tofu with a small piece of baking paper and another oven tray. Place cans of food on top to weight, then refrigerate for 1 hour to drain. Pat tofu dry with paper towel and slice thinly lengthways. Divide between two large oven trays lined with baking paper. Combine remaining ingredients in a small bowl; season with black pepper. Brush both sides of tofu with miso mixture. Cover and refrigerate overnight.

TRY THIS

Use in wholegrain rolls with thinly shaved fennel and carrot, fresh coriander, mint and finely chopped chilli for a vegan tofu bánh mì.

Stirred into egg-based dishes: such as scrambled eggs, omelettes and frittatas.

Scattered over soups or stews for an added protein hit.

TIPS The tofu bacon
recipe makes double
the amount required
for this recipe but
it will keep uncooked
in the fridge for
up to 1 week; just
bake as required.
For other uses, see
'try this' opposite.

TIPS You will need approximately 3 medium (360g) carrots. Manchego is a semi-firm Spanish sheep's milk cheese available from major supermarkets and delis. Substitute with mature cheddar, if you like. Use an old yet clean tea towel for squeezing the grated carrot, as it may stain.

CARROT TACO SHELLS WITH CHIPOTLE PORK

PREP + COOK TIME **40 MINUTES (+ STANDING)** MAKES **4**

- 2 teaspoons olive oil
- 250g (8 ounces) minced (ground) pork
- 1 finely chopped chipotle chilli in adobo sauce, plus 2 teaspoons adobo sauce, optional
- ½ cup (140g) Greek-style yoghurt
- 40g (1½ ounces) gem lettuce leaves, shredded
- 1 medium avocado (250g), sliced thinly
- 2 tablespoons lime juice
- 1 small red onion (100g), sliced thinly
- 20g (¾ ounce) snow pea shoots
- 1 lime, cut into wedges
- extra gem lettuce leaves, to serve
- no-nasties chilli sauce (see page 69), to serve

CARROT TACO SHELLS

- 1½ cups (230g) coarsely grated carrot (see tips)
- ½ cup (60g) grated manchego cheese
- 2 eggs, beaten lightly
- ¼ cup (35g) oat flour

1 Preheat oven to 200°C/400°F. Line two oven trays with baking paper.

2 Make carrot taco shells.

3 Meanwhile, heat oil in a large frying pan over high heat. Cook pork, breaking up any lumps with a spoon, for 5 minutes or until browned and cooked through. Add chilli; cook for a further 1 minute. Season to taste.

4 Swirl reserved adobo sauce, if using, through yoghurt. Divide shredded lettuce, pork mixture, avocado, combined lime juice and onion, yoghurt mixture and pea shoots evenly among taco shells. Serve with lime wedges, extra lettuce leaves and no-nasties chilli sauce.

CARROT TACO SHELLS

Steam or boil carrot for 3 minutes or until tender. Place in a tea towel (see tips) and squeeze to remove excess liquid. Place in a medium bowl with cheese, egg and flour; stir to combine. Season. Divide carrot mixture into quarters; spread out into four 14cm (5½-inch) rounds on trays. Bake taco shells for 20 minutes or until golden; stand on trays for 1 minute. Taking care as shells will still be warm, bend each round over a small bottle to form a taco shape. Leave to cool on bottle.

NO·FRY·STIR·FRY WITH COCONUT NAM JIM

PREP TIME **25 MINUTES** SERVES **2**

- 2 small heads broccoli (500g)
- 200g (7 ounces) daikon, julienned
- 1 medium purple carrot (120g), julienned
- 1 green mango (350g), peeled, julienned
- 60g (2 ounces) asparagus, peeled lengthways into long ribbons
- ½ cup (75g) roasted cashews, chopped coarsely
- ¼ cup fresh thai basil leaves
- ¼ cup fresh coriander (cilantro) leaves

COCONUT NAM JIM

- 2 fresh long green chillies, seeded, chopped
- 2 shallots (50g), peeled, chopped coarsely
- 2 cloves garlic, chopped coarsely
- 2 tablespoons fresh coriander (cilantro) leaves
- ¼ cup (60ml) lime juice
- ¼ cup (60ml) coconut cream
- 1 tablespoon fish sauce
- 1 tablespoon raw honey

1 Make coconut nam jim.

2 Using a sharp knife; chop broccoli heads into very small pieces. Trim broccoli stems; using a julienne peeler, peel stems into long, thin matchsticks. (Alternatively, use a sharp knife.) Transfer all broccoli to a large bowl.

3 Add remaining ingredients to bowl, drizzle with coconut nam jim; toss to combine. Serve immediately.

COCONUT NAM JIM

Blend or process ingredients until smooth. (Makes 1¼ cups)

SWAP OUT the purple carrot for a regular medium orange carrot, if that is what's in your fridge.

KEEPS Store coconut nam jim in an airtight jar in the fridge for up to 3 days; shake before using.

TIPS A julienne peeler looks like a regular wide peeler, except it has wide serrations to make easy work of cutting vegetables into julienne. They are available from kitchen supply stores and Asian grocers. Use to cut the daikon, carrot and mango, as well as the broccoli into julienne.

TIPS Make sure you purchase sun-dried tomatoes without brine, oil or any other liquid, as you need the dried version for this recipe to soak up some of the vegetable juices released during cooking. You can fry any leftover sage leaves in a little olive oil until crisp, then use to garnish the lasagne, if you like.

* This clever vegetarian lasagne stars vegetables
in different ways. Eggplant and zucchini replace
pasta, while mushrooms and tomato combine for a
hearty tomato sauce, and cauliflower and ricotta
are transformed into a silky béchamel.

EGGPLANT AND ZUCCHINI LASAGNE

PREP + COOK TIME **1 HOUR 30 MINUTES (+ STANDING & COOLING)** SERVES **6**

- ⅓ cup (80ml) extra virgin olive oil
- 2 eggplants (600g)
- 3 large zucchini (450g)
- 200g (7 ounces) fresh shiitake mushrooms, stems discarded, chopped finely
- 2 tablespoons finely chopped sage
- 1 teaspoon smoked paprika
- 400g (12½ ounces) canned chopped tomatoes
- 125g (4 ounces) sun-dried tomatoes, chopped finely (see tips)
- ¾ cup (90g) walnuts, chopped finely
- 1 cup (250ml) tomato passata
- 1 cup (250ml) vegetable stock
- ¼ cup (20g) finely grated parmesan

CAULIFLOWER BÉCHAMEL

- ¾ head cauliflower (750g), cut into florets
- 3 cloves garlic, bruised
- 1½ cups (375ml) vegetable stock
- 375g (12 ounces) fresh ricotta
- ¾ cup (60g) finely grated parmesan
- ¼ teaspoon ground nutmeg

1 Preheat oven grill to high. Line a large oven tray with foil; grease with oil.

2 Cut eggplant and zucchini lengthways into 4mm (⅛-inch) thick slices.

3 Place eggplant, in batches, in a single layer on oiled tray; brush with 1 tablespoon of the oil and season. Grill eggplant slices for 5 minutes each side or until golden. Repeat with zucchini slices and another 1 tablespoon of oil; grill for 3 minutes each side or until golden.

4 Preheat oven on 200°C/400°F.

5 Make cauliflower béchamel.

6 Meanwhile, heat 1 tablespoon of the oil in a frying pan over medium-high heat. Cook mushroom for 2 minutes, add sage and paprika; cook for a further 3 minutes or until golden. Stir in canned and dried tomatoes, walnuts, passata and stock to combine, bring to a simmer; simmer for 12 minutes or until thickened slightly. Season to taste.

7 Spread a quarter of the cauliflower bechamel in a 2.5 litre (10-cup) rectangular baking dish; arrange a layer of vegetables over. Top with another quarter of the bechamel. Spoon over half of sun-dried tomato mixture, then repeat layering with vegetables, bechamel and tomato mixture, finishing with remaining béchamel. Top with parmesan; drizzle with remaining oil and season with salt and pepper.

8 Bake for 20 minutes or until top is golden and filling heated through. Stand for 10 minutes before serving.

CAULIFLOWER BÉCHAMEL

Place cauliflower, garlic and stock in a medium saucepan over medium heat; bring to a simmer. Reduce heat to low; cook, covered, for 12 minutes or until cauliflower is tender. Cool for 10 minutes. Blend with cheeses and nutmeg until a smooth puree forms; season.

✳ This is a vegetarian play on the classic pasta and meatball theme, except in our version, there's neither meat nor pasta. Beans, walnuts and fetta all combine to make luscious, hearty 'meatballs', while zucchini fills the role of pasta - together they provide a good dose of your daily vegetable, protein and calcium needs.

'SPAGHETTI' AND 'MEATBALLS'

PREP + COOK TIME **45 MINUTES** SERVES **4**

- 400g (12½ ounces) canned butter beans, drained, rinsed
- 100g (3 ounces) walnut pieces, chopped finely
- 1 egg
- ½ cup fresh basil leaves, chopped coarsely
- 2 garlic cloves, chopped finely
- ⅓ cup (50g) chickpea flour (besan)
- 120g (4 ounces) greek fetta, crumbled
- ¼ cup (60ml) extra virgin olive oil
- 2 x 400g (12½ ounces) canned chopped tomatoes
- ½ cup (125ml) vegetable stock or water
- 4 large zucchini (600g), spiralised into spaghetti (see tip)

1 Place beans in a large bowl; mash lightly with a fork. Add walnuts, egg, half of the basil, garlic, flour and ½ cup of the fetta; stir until combined. Season generously to taste.

2 Using damp hands, roll bean mixture into 4cm (1½-inch) balls.

3 Heat 1 tablespoon of the oil in a large frying pan over medium heat. Cook 'meatballs', turning frequently, for 5 minutes or until browned.

4 Add tomatoes, stock and remaining oil to pan with 'meatballs'; season well. Cook for 15 minutes or until sauce thickens and reduces slightly and 'meatballs' are coated.

5 Meanwhile, place zucchini in a large sieve or colander over a large heatproof bowl. Pour over boiling water to soften. Drain and set aside.

6 Top zucchini 'spaghetti' with 'meatball' mixture; sprinkle with remaining fetta and basil. Season to taste.

TIP Spiralisers
are available
from kitchen and
homeware stores.
Alternatively, you
can cut the zucchini
into julienne
(matchsticks), using
a mandoline or a
very sharp knife.

TIP Black rice is available from supermarkets. It has a nutty taste and slightly firmer texture than white rice. Once cooked, it takes on a purple hue. Substitute with cooked quinoa, if you like.

SIMPLE SATAY SALAD JARS

PREP + COOK TIME **1 HOUR 15 MINUTES** SERVES **4**

- ½ bunch kale (150g)
- 2 teaspoons olive oil
- ⅓ cup (50g) black rice (see tips)
- 2 tablespoons coconut oil
- 1 shallot, chopped finely
- 1 clove garlic, crushed
- 2 teaspoons finely grated fresh ginger
- 1 fresh small red chilli, seeded, chopped finely
- ½ cup (140g) smooth peanut butter
- 1 tablespoon tamari
- 2 teaspoons honey
- 270ml can coconut milk
- 2 tablespoons lime juice
- 300g (9½ ounces) soft tofu, crumbled
- ¼ medium red cabbage (160g), shredded thinly
- 1 large carrot (180g), julienned

1 Preheat oven to 120°C/250°F fan-forced. Line an oven tray with baking paper.

2 Tear leaves from kale, toss with olive oil; season to taste. Place on tray; roast for 30 minutes or until dry and crisp.

3 Meanwhile, cook rice in a saucepan of boiling salted water for 35 minutes or until tender; drain.

4 Heat 1 tablespoon of the coconut oil in a small saucepan over medium heat. Cook shallot, garlic, ginger and chilli, stirring, for 2 minutes or until soft. Stir in peanut butter, tamari and honey until smooth. Add coconut milk and lime juice; stir to combine. Simmer gently over low heat for 5 minutes or until thickened.

5 Heat remaining coconut oil in a small saucepan over high heat. Add tofu; cook, stirring continuously, for 5 minutes or until warmed through. Season to taste.

6 Layer satay sauce, cabbage, tofu, rice and carrot evenly in four 1-cup (250ml) jars. Serve topped with crisp kale.

SUPER GREENS CHICKEN SALAD

PREP + COOK TIME **1 HOUR 10 MINUTES** SERVES **2**

For four or six people, simply double or triple the recipe to suit your needs.

- 175g (5½ ounces) broccolini
- 220g (7 ounces) green beans, halved lengthways
- 110g (3½ ounces) snow peas
- 3 cups (750ml) water
- 2 cloves garlic
- 2cm (¾-inch) piece fresh ginger, sliced
- 200g (6½-ounce) chicken breast fillet
- 1½ tablespoons matcha (green tea) powder

WASABI PUFFS

- 1 egg white
- 1 tablespoon tamari
- 1 teaspoon wasabi paste
- ¼ teaspoon sea salt flakes
- 1 cup (35g) puffed rice
- 1 cup (140g) slivered almonds
- 1 tablespoon black sesame seeds
- 1 nori (seaweed) sheet, cut into thin strips (see tips)

AVOCADO DRESSING

- 1 medium avocado (250g)
- 3 teaspoons unhulled tahini
- 1½ tablespoons olive oil
- 1½ tablespoons lime juice
- 1 teaspoon sesame oil

1 Make wasabi puffs.

2 Cook broccolini and beans in a saucepan of boiling water for 3 minutes; add snow peas, cook for a further 1 minute or until vegetables are just tender. Drain, cool under cold running water; drain.

3 Place the water, garlic and ginger in a small saucepan; bring to the boil. Add chicken, return to the boil; reduce heat to low. Add matcha; cook, covered, for 10 minutes or until chicken is cooked through. Cool chicken in liquid for 10 minutes; remove and slice thinly. Discard the cooking liquid.

4 Meanwhile, make avocado dressing.

5 Arrange vegetables and chicken on a platter or large plate, top with a generous spoonful of avocado dressing; scatter with wasabi puffs. Serve with remaining dressing separate.

WASABI PUFFS

Preheat oven to 150°C/300°F. Line an oven tray with baking paper. Whisk egg white, tamari, wasabi and salt in a small bowl until combined. Place rice, almonds and seeds in a medium bowl; pour over wet mixture. Spread mixture evenly over lined oven tray. Roast for 20 minutes or until crisp. Cool; stir in nori.

AVOCADO DRESSING

Process all ingredients until combined and as smooth as possible. Season to taste.
(Makes ¾ cup)

KEEPS Store wasabi puffs in an airtight container in the pantry for up to 2 weeks.

TIPS The easiest way to cut nori sheets is with a pair of kitchen scissors. Leftover wasabi puffs can be sprinkled over steamed vegetables, an omelette or a fried egg.

TIPS The coconut oil
needs to be at room
temperature for the
pastry to combine.
If it has been in the
fridge, leave it at
room temperature for
1 hour to soften.

CREAMY MUSHROOM AND KALE POT PIES

PREP + COOK TIME 1 HOUR 30 MINUTES (+ REFRIGERATION) SERVES 4

- 1 tablespoon olive oil
- 1 leek (350g), sliced thinly
- 200g (6½ ounces) swiss brown mushrooms, quartered
- 4 medium portobello mushrooms (200g), chopped coarsely
- 1 clove garlic, sliced thinly
- 60g (2 ounces) kale leaves, chopped coarsely
- ½ cup coarsely chopped fresh flat-leaf parsley
- 1 teaspoon finely grated lemon rind
- 2 teaspoons lemon juice
- 1 egg, beaten lightly
- 1 teaspoon sesame seeds
- ½ teaspoon fennel seeds, chopped coarsely
- ½ teaspoon sea salt flakes

SPELT PASTRY
- 1⅓ cups (200g) plain (all-purpose) spelt flour
- ¼ teaspoon fine sea salt
- ½ cup (120g) coconut oil, at room temperature
- 1 tablespoon iced water, approximately

WHITE SAUCE
- 1 cup (250ml) milk
- 1 small cauliflower (750g), chopped finely
- 1 cup (80g) grated parmesan

1 Make spelt pastry.

2 Meanwhile, make white sauce.

3 Preheat oven to 180°C/350°F. Place four 10cm (4¾-inch) round, 1¼-cup (310ml) ovenproof dishes on an oven tray.

4 Heat oil in a large frying pan over medium heat. Add leek; cook, stirring, for 5 minutes or until soft. Add mushroom and garlic; cook, stirring, for 10 minutes or until tender and liquid is evaporated. Stir through kale; cook for a further 1 minute or until just wilted. Remove from heat; stir in parsley, rind and juice; season to taste.

5 Combine mushroom mixture and white sauce in a large bowl; divide among dishes.

6 Roll out pastry between two sheets of baking paper until 3mm (⅛-inch) thick. Cut out four 12cm (4¾-inch) rounds from pastry. Cover dishes with pastry rounds, pressing around edges to seal. Brush tops with egg; sprinkle with combined seeds and sea salt.

7 Bake pot pies for 30 minutes or until pastry is golden.

SPELT PASTRY
Sift flour and salt into a large bowl. Using a teaspoon, scoop up spoonfuls of the coconut oil; scrape off with a second teaspoon into the bowl. Using your fingertips, rub into flour until mixture resembles wet sand. Add the iced water, a little at a time, stirring with a butter knife, until a dough forms. Gently knead on a lightly floured work surface for 30 seconds or until smooth. Enclose in plastic wrap; refrigerate for 10 minutes.

WHITE SAUCE
Place milk and cauliflower in a medium saucepan. Cover, bring to a simmer, reduce heat to low-medium; cook, covered, for 8 minutes or until cauliflower is just tender. Cool slightly. Blend cauliflower mixture and parmesan until smooth; season to taste.

BASIC SHAKSHUKA

PREP + COOK TIME **25 MINUTES** SERVES **2**

- 8 stems fresh flat-leaf parsley
- 2 tablespoons olive oil
- 1 medium onion (150g), chopped finely
- 2 cloves garlic, crushed
- 1½ teaspoons sea salt flakes
- 1 teaspoon cracked black pepper
- 1½ teaspoons ground cumin
- 1½ teaspoons smoked paprika
- 800g (1½ pounds) canned tomatoes
- 4 eggs

1 Finely chop the stalks of the parsley. Heat oil in a large 28cm (11¼-inch) wide, 26cm (10½-inch) base frying pan, over medium heat. Add chopped stalks, onion, garlic, salt, pepper and spices; cook, stirring for 3 minutes or until soft. Add tomatoes; reduce heat to low, simmer for 8 minutes.

2 Make four indents in the sauce and break in eggs; season. Reduce heat to low; cook, covered, for 6 minutes or until eggs are just set.

3 Meanwhile, chop parsley leaves; sprinkle over shakshuka.

SERVE WITH chargrilled sourdough bread, if you like.

GREEN GOODNESS
SHAKSHUKA

White bean shakshuka
with avocado

GREEN GOODNESS SHAKSHUKA
PREP + COOK TIME **25 MINUTES** SERVES **2**

Preheat grill (broiler) to high. Cut white stems from 800g (1½lbs) silver beet, discard; chop leaves coarsely. Heat 2 tablespoons olive oil and 20g (¾oz) butter in a 28cm (11¼-in) wide, 26cm (10½-in) base frying pan over medium heat. Add 1 sliced leek, 2 cloves crushed garlic, silver beet leaves, 2 tablespoons chopped flat-leaf parsley stalks, 1½ teaspoons each ground cumin and smoked paprika; cook, stirring, for 6 minutes or until silver beet is tender. Make four indents in silver beet mixture; break in 4 eggs and season. Reduce heat to low; cook, covered, for 3 minutes or until eggs begin to set. Sprinkle with 100g (3oz) crumbled fetta and 2 tablespoons pine nuts. Place under grill; cook for 3 minutes or until eggs are set and fetta is browned. Sprinkle with ⅓ cup crumbled fetta, 2 tablespoons coarsely chopped fresh flat-leaf parsley and 1 thinly sliced green onion (scallion); season.

SPICY EGGPLANT SHAKSHUKA
PREP + COOK TIME **25 MINUTES** SERVES **2**

Cut 1 medium eggplant into 1cm (¾-in) cubes. Heat ½ cup olive oil in a 28cm (11¼-in) wide, 26cm (10½-in) base frying pan over medium heat. Add eggplant, 2 tablespoons finely chopped flat-leaf parsley stalks, 1 finely chopped medium onion, 2 cloves crushed garlic, ½ teaspoon chilli flakes and 1½ teaspoons each ground cumin and smoked paprika. Cook, stirring, for 6 minutes or until eggplant is soft. Add 800g (1½lb) canned tomatoes, reduce heat to low; simmer for 8 minutes, stirring occasionally. Make four indents in eggplant mixture; break in 4 eggs and season to taste. Reduce heat to low. Cook, covered, for 6 minutes or until eggs begin to set. Process ½ cup plain Greek-style yoghurt, ¼ cup chopped fresh flat-leaf parsley and 2 pickled japaleño chillies in a small food processor until smooth. Drizzle over shakshuka, top with 2 tablespoons chopped fresh flat-leaf parsley; season.

WHITE BEAN SHAKSHUKA WITH AVOCADO
PREP + COOK TIME **25 MINUTES** SERVES **2**

Make shakshuka using the ingredients and method for basic recipe (see page 108), except: substitute ½ teaspoon crushed fennel seeds for smoked paprika; fresh coriander (cilantro) for parsley; and add 400g (12½oz), canned cannellini beans, drained and rinsed, with the tomatoes. While shakshuka is cooking, dice flesh from 1 medium avocado; combine with 1 tablespoon lime juice. Top shakshuka with avocado mixture and 1 tablespoon coarsely chopped fresh coriander (cilantro); season.

SPICY EGGPLANT
SHAKSHUKA

GINGER CHICKEN WITH RAW CITRUS RIBBON SALAD

PREP + COOK TIME **30 MINUTES (+ REFRIGERATION & COOLING)** SERVES **2**

- 2 chicken breast fillets (500g)
- 2 tablespoons vegetable oil
- 1 large zucchini (150g)
- 1 large carrot (180g)
- 3 target beetroot (350g), sliced thinly
- 1 cup (60g) bean sprouts
- ¼ cup (40g) roasted cashews
- 1 green onion (scallion), sliced thinly
- ½ small red grapefruit (175g)
- 1 lime (65g), halved

MARINADE

- ¼ cup (60ml) soy sauce
- 1 tablespoon pure maple syrup
- 2 cloves garlic
- 2 teaspoons finely grated fresh ginger
- ½ teaspoon ground coriander
- ¼ cup fresh coriander (cilantro) stalks
- 2 tablespoons lime juice

DRESSING

- 1 tablespoon pure maple syrup
- ⅓ cup (50g) roasted cashews
- 1 teaspoon finely grated fresh ginger
- ½ fresh long red chilli, seeded
- 2 tablespoons lime juice
- 1 tablespoon soy sauce
- ½ cup fresh coriander (cilantro) leaves

1 Make marinade.

2 Place chicken in a medium bowl; pour over marinade. Cover with plastic wrap; refrigerate for at least 2 hours or overnight. Drain; discard marinade.

3 Heat oil in a medium frying pan over medium heat. Cook chicken for 4 minutes each side or until golden and cooked through. Transfer to a plate; cool for 10 minutes. Slice thickly.

4 Make dressing.

5 Using a vegetable peeler, slice zucchini and carrot into long ribbons. Place vegetable ribbons, beetroot, bean sprouts, cashews and green onion on a large platter.

6 Using a small sharp knife, cut away rind and white pith from grapefruit and one lime half. Cut between citrus membranes to release segments; add to salad.

7 Top salad with sliced chicken, drizzle with dressing; season to taste. Slice remaining half lime in two; serve salad with lime and remaining dressing.

MARINADE

Process all ingredients until smooth.

DRESSING

Process all ingredients until as smooth as possible.

SWAP OUT If red grapefruit is unavailable, replace with navel orange or blood orange segments. Squeeze the citrus membranes to yield 2 tablespoons juice, then use in the dressing instead of lime juice.

LAMB AND WALNUT PITTAS WITH TURKISH SALAD

PREP + COOK TIME **35 MINUTES** SERVES **4**

- 2 tablespoons olive oil
- 250g (8 ounces) minced (ground) lamb
- 2 teaspoons cumin seeds
- 1 clove garlic, crushed
- 3 teaspoons finely chopped fresh rosemary
- ⅓ cup (35g) coarsely chopped walnuts
- ¾ cup (195g) tomato passata
- 4 wholemeal pitta pocket breads
- ½ cup (140g) Greek-style yoghurt
- 2 tablespoons fresh flat-leaf parsley
- 1 tablespoon fresh mint leaves
- 4 lemon wedges

TURKISH SALAD
- 1 cup loosely packed fresh flat-leaf parsley leaves
- 1 cup loosely packed fresh mint leaves
- ¼ cup (40g) pomegranate seeds
- ½ small red onion (50g), sliced thinly
- 80g (2½ ounces) fetta, crumbled

1 Preheat oven to 220°C/425°F. Line two oven trays with baking paper.

2 Heat 1 tablespoon oil in a medium frying pan over high heat. Add lamb, cumin, garlic, rosemary and walnuts; cook, breaking up any lumps with a wooden spoon, for 5 minutes or until browned. Add passata; cook for 1 minute or until warmed through. Season to taste.

3 Place pitta breads on trays, top evenly with lamb mixture; drizzle with remaining oil. Bake pittas for 10 minutes or until crisp and golden.

4 Make turkish salad.

5 Process yoghurt and herbs until smooth; season to taste. Top pittas with salad, drizzle with yoghurt mixture and serve with lemon wedges.

TURKISH SALAD
Combine all ingredients in a medium bowl. Season to taste.

SUGAR ALERT! Check the pitta bread packet label for sugar amounts. Authentic pitta includes an absolute minimum of sugar, while widely available commercial brands include more. Tomato passata is pureed and sieved Italian tomatoes. Sold in bottles, it contains no added sugar, unlike bottled pasta sauce.

✳ Easy, fresh and vibrant, this recipe is the
perfect weeknight dinner meal solution, proving that
fish really is fast to cook. Make double the salad
and take it to work the next day in a sandwich. We used
four baby golden beetroot and four target beetroot,
and sliced the vegetables thinly with a mandoline.

BEETROOT, COCONUT AND SEED SALAD WITH SNAPPER

PREP + COOK TIME **25 MINUTES** SERVES **4**

- ⅓ cup (50g) sunflower seeds
- ¼ cup (60ml) extra virgin olive oil
- 1 tablespoon lemon juice
- 1 teaspoon dijon mustard
- 1 teaspoon honey
- 4 x 200g (7-ounce) snapper fillets
- 1 teaspoon ground cumin

- 8 mixed baby beetroot (beets) (25g), sliced thinly
- 4 watermelon radishes (35g), sliced thinly
- ½ cup fresh small mint leaves
- ½ cup (40g) shaved coconut
- 1 lemon (140g), cut into wedges

1 Heat a small frying pan over medium heat; cook sunflower seeds, stirring
continuously, for 2 minutes or until toasted; remove from pan.
2 Whisk 2 tablespoons of the olive oil, the juice, mustard and honey in a small
bowl until well combined. Season to taste.
3 Heat a medium non-stick frying pan over medium-high heat. Brush snapper fillets
with remaining olive oil; sprinkle with cumin and season with salt and pepper.
Cook fish, skin-side down, for 2 minutes; turn and cook for a further 2 minutes
or until fish is cooked through.
4 Combine beetroot and radish with half each of the mint and sunflower seeds
and the dressing in a medium bowl.
5 Divide salad among plates; scatter with remaining sunflower seeds and mint.
Top each with a snapper fillet; serve with shaved coconut and lemon wedges.

SWAP OUT For a vegetarian option, swap the fish for crumbled goat's cheese.

TIPS Whiting and
john dory are good
alternatives to
snapper fillets.
You could also serve
the salad with pan-
fried or grilled
chicken or lamb.

✳ Fresh herbs aren't often thought of as sources
of nutrients, but should be. Fresh coriander
leaves have good antioxidant properties and are
a rich source of vitamin K, a fat-soluble vitamin
best known for the role it plays in blood clotting.

ROAST SALMON WITH SPICED LENTILS AND DILL YOGHURT

PREP + COOK TIME **45 MINUTES** SERVES **2**

- ⅓ cup (80g) French-style green lentils
- 8 cups (2 litres) water
- 400g (12½-ounce) piece boneless salmon fillet, skin on
- ¼ cup (60ml) olive oil
- 2 medium lemons (140g)
- 1 teaspoon sea salt flakes
- 1 teaspoon cracked black pepper
- 1 medium onion (150g), chopped finely
- 2 cloves garlic, crushed
- 2 teaspoons ground cumin
- 2 teaspoons ground coriander
- 100g (3 ounces) baby spinach
- ½ cup fresh coriander (cilantro) leaves
- 2 tablespoons finely chopped dill
- ½ cup (140g) Greek-style yoghurt
- lemon cheeks and dill sprigs, to serve

1 Preheat oven to 200°C/400°F. Line an oven tray with baking paper.

2 Place lentils and the water in a large saucepan over medium-high heat. Bring to the boil. Reduce heat to medium; simmer lentils for 20 minutes or until tender. Drain.

3 Place salmon, skin-side down, on oven tray; rub 1 tablespoon of the oil over salmon fillets. Finely grate rind of 1 lemon over salmon; sprinkle with ½ teaspoon of the salt and ½ teaspoon of the pepper. Roast for 7 minutes or until almost cooked but slightly pink in the centre. Cut salmon in half lengthways.

4 Meanwhile, heat remaining oil in a medium frying pan over medium heat. Cook onion, garlic and spices, stirring for 3 minutes or until lightly golden. Add lentils to pan; cook, covered, for 1 minute. Remove pan from heat.

5 Juice 1 lemon into a medium bowl. Add lentil mixture, spinach, coriander and remaining salt and pepper; mix well.

6 Juice remaining lemon into a small bowl. Add dill and yoghurt; whisk to combine. Season to taste.

7 Divide lentil mixture between plates; top with salmon and drizzle with yoghurt mixture. Season to taste. Serve with lemon cheeks, sprinkled with dill sprigs.

SWAP OUT the salmon for a skinless, boneless ocean trout fillet and the spinach for rocket, if you like.

✳ Tomatoes are acidic, so balancing out their flavour
with something sweet is helpful. We've used stevia, rather
than table sugar, to balance out the flavours of the stew.

FISH AND FENNEL STEW

PREP + COOK TIME **45 MINUTES** SERVES **4**

- ¼ cup (60ml) extra virgin olive oil
- 1 medium onion (150g),
  chopped finely
- 2 medium fennel bulbs (600g),
  fronds reserved, sliced thinly
- 2 cloves garlic, crushed
- 1 fresh long red chilli,
  sliced thinly
- ½ cup (125ml) dry white wine
- 3 cups (750ml) fish stock or broth
  (see page 61)
- 800g (1½ pounds) canned diced
  tomatoes

- ¼ teaspoon liquid stevia or
  unrefined sugar, optional
- 750g (1½ pounds) boneless white
  fish fillets, cut into
  3cm (1¼-inch) pieces
- 2 tablespoons coarsely chopped
  fresh flat-leaf parsley
- 4 slices seeded sourdough bread
  (280g)
- 2 teaspoons finely grated
  lemon rind
- 1 medium lemon (140g),
  cut into cheeks

1 Heat 1½ tablespoons of the olive oil in a large saucepan over medium heat.
Add onion and fennel; cook, stirring, for 5 minutes or until soft. Add garlic
and chilli; cook for 1 minute or until fragrant.

2 Add wine; bring to the boil. Add stock, tomatoes and stevia; bring to the boil.
Reduce heat to low-medium; cook, covered, for 20 minutes. Season to taste.
Add fish cook, covered, stirring occasionally, for a further 5 minutes or until
fish is cooked through. Stir in parsley.

3 Just before serving, preheat a chargrill pan over medium heat. Brush bread
with remaining olive oil; cook for 1 minute each side or until golden and
lightly charred.

4 Top stew with lemon rind and reserved fennel fronds. Serve with grilled
sourdough and lemon cheeks.

TIPS We used snapper here. You could add extra seafood to the stew, such as uncooked prawns and mussels.

TIP The hotter the pan, the easier the dosa mixture is to work with. A good quality non-stick frying pan lined with a round of baking paper gives the best results.

POTATO, SPINACH AND CHICKPEA CURRY WITH CORIANDER DOSA

PREP + COOK TIME **1 HOUR** SERVES **6**

- ¼ cup (60g) ghee
- 1 medium onion (150g), sliced thinly
- 1 clove garlic, crushed
- 1 fresh long red chilli, seeded, sliced thinly
- 2 teaspoons finely grated ginger
- 2 teaspoons black mustard seeds
- 2 teaspoons cumin seeds
- 1 teaspoon ground turmeric
- 3 medium tomatoes (450g), diced
- 1kg (2 pounds) potatoes, peeled, cut into 2cm (¾-inch) pieces
- ⅓ cup (80ml) water
- 1 bunch spinach (300g), chopped coarsely
- coriander sprigs, to serve

CORIANDER DOSA

- 1 cup (150g) chickpea flour (besan)
- 2 cups (500ml) room-temperature water
- 2 tablespoons lemon juice
- ¼ cup coarsely chopped fresh coriander (cilantro)

1 Heat 1½ tablespoons of the ghee in a medium saucepan over medium-high heat; cook onion, stirring, for 5 minutes or until soft. Add garlic, chilli, ginger and spices; cook, stirring, for 1 minute or until fragrant.

2 Add tomato to pan; cook, stirring, for 2 minutes or until softened. Add potato and the water; stir to coat in mixture. Cook, covered, over low-medium heat, stirring frequently, for 35 minutes or until potato is tender.

3 Meanwhile, make coriander dosa.

4 Just before serving, stir spinach into curry; cook for a further 3 minutes or until wilted. Season to taste.

5 Top curry with coriander sprigs; serve with coriander dosa.

CORIANDER DOSA

Whisk chickpea flour, the water and lemon juice in a medium bowl until a smooth, thin batter forms. Add a little extra water, if necessary to achieve the desired consistency. Stir in coriander. Heat 1 teaspoon ghee in a large 25cm (10-inch) wide, 22cm (9-inch) base non-stick frying pan or crêpe pan lined with a round of baking paper over high heat. Add ⅓ cup of batter to pan, swirling pan to cover base evenly; cook for 1½ minutes or until bubbles appear on the surface and dosa is golden underneath. Turn with a spatula; cook for a further 1 minute or until golden. Transfer to a plate. Repeat with remaining ghee and batter to make 6 dosa in total.

QUICK FIXES

FROZEN TAHINI, BLACK SESAME AND COCONUT FUDGE

PREP + COOK TIME **15 MINUTES (+ FREEZING)** MAKES **18**

- 1 cup (250ml) coconut cream
- ⅓ cup (80ml) hulled tahini
- 2 tablespoons pure maple syrup
- 1 teaspoon pure vanilla extract
- pinch sea salt
- 2 tablespoons coconut oil
- 1 teaspoon mesquite powder, optional (see tip)
- 1 teaspoon black sesame seeds

1 Grease a 10cm x 20cm (4-inch x 8-inch) loaf pan; line base and sides with baking paper.
2 Process coconut cream, tahini, syrup, vanilla, salt, coconut oil and mesquite powder, if using, until mixture is smooth.
3 Pour into tin; sprinkle with sesame seeds. Freeze for 2 hours or until set.
4 Using an oiled knife, cut into 18 pieces.

KEEPS Store in an airtight container in the freezer for up to 2 weeks. Stand at room temperature for 10 minutes to soften before serving.

TIP Mesquite powder is made from the extract of mesquite plant seeds indigenous to North and South America. Appreciated for its sweet, caramel-like flavour, it is rich in minerals and protein. It is available from health food stores.

TIPS Spirulina is a nutrient-rich sea algae, packed with minerals, B-vitamins and iron. It is advisable to buy it in smallish quantities, as it is thought that the nutritional benefits can diminish after about 3 months of opening. It is available from major supermarkets and health food stores. You could also serve this recipe with a spinach and watercress salad to make it a more substantial meal.

✳ You may need to turn the fan on in your oven for the last 5-10 minutes of cooking, if you find that the vegies aren't browning enough. Spirulina is by no means essential to the guacamole but is a way of boosting your green vegie intake if you have it on hand.

HEALTHY VEGIE FRIES WITH SUPER-FOOD GUACAMOLE

PREP + COOK TIME **1 HOUR** SERVES **4**

- 1 large orange sweet potato (500g)
- 2 large parsnips (700g)
- ¼ cup (60ml) extra virgin olive oil

SUPER-FOOD GUACAMOLE

- 2 medium avocados (500g)
- 1 fresh small red chilli, chopped finely
- 1 small clove garlic, crushed
- 1 tablespoon lime juice
- ½ cup finely chopped fresh coriander (cilantro)
- ¼ teaspoon spirulina

1 Preheat oven to 220°C/440°F. Line two large oven trays with baking paper.
2 Scrub vegetables; pat dry with paper towel. Cut unpeeled vegetables into 1cm (½-inch) thick fries. Place vegetables in a medium bowl, drizzle with olive oil; toss to coat well.
3 Spread vegetables in a single layer evenly over oven trays. Season to taste with salt.
4 Bake vegetables, turning halfway through cooking, for 45 minutes or until golden and tender.

5 Meanwhile, make super-food guacamole.
6 Serve warm vegie fries with super-food guacamole.

SUPER-FOOD GUACAMOLE

Mash avocado in a medium bowl. Add remaining ingredients, mix well; season to taste.

CACAO BOMBS WITH PASSIONFRUIT

PREP + COOK TIME **25 MINUTES (+ REFRIGERATION & FREEZING)** MAKES **15**

- 4 fresh dates (80g), pitted
- ¼ cup (60ml) boiling water
- 60g (2 ounces) cacao butter, chopped coarsely (see tips)
- ¼ cup (55g) coconut oil, solid (see tips)
- 2 tablespoons cacao powder
- 1 tablespoon pure maple syrup
- 2 pinches sea salt
- ¼ teaspoon pure vanilla extract
- 3 passionfruit, pulp removed

1 Place dates in a small bowl; cover with boiling water. Set aside for 15 minutes. Place 15 mini-patty paper cases on a large oven tray.

2 Place cacao butter, coconut oil, cacao powder, syrup and a pinch of salt in a small saucepan over medium heat; stir until melted and combined.

3 Divide half of the chocolate mixture evenly among paper cases, using 1½ teaspoons for each one. Reserve remaining chocolate mixture to use later. Place in freezer for 10 minutes or until set.

4 Drain dates, reserving 1 tablespoon of the soaking water. Process dates, reserved water, vanilla and a pinch of salt until smooth. Spoon ½ teaspoon of the date caramel into centre of each patty case; top evenly with remaining chocolate mixture.

5 Refrigerate for at least 1 hour or until chocolate mixture is set; freeze. Serve topped with passionfruit pulp.

KEEPS Store in an airtight container in the freezer for up to 2 weeks.

TIPS The coconut oil
needs to be solid
for this recipe.
If you can't find
cacao butter you
can substitute
cocoa butter.

TIP The time it
takes to dry the kale
may differ depending
on the size of the
torn pieces.

✳ Think of this recipe as more than just a snack. Try using it as a topper for soups, salads and egg dishes.

KALE CHIPS WITH SESAME AND CORIANDER

PREP + COOK TIME **1 HOUR** SERVES **4 (MAKES 6 CUPS)**

- ¼ cup (70g) unhulled tahini
- 2 teaspoons ground coriander
- 1 tablespoon extra virgin olive oil
- 2 tablespoons sesame seeds
- 1 teaspoon sea salt flakes
- 1 bunch green kale (250g), stems removed, discarded

1 Preheat oven to 120°C/250°F fan-forced. Line two large oven trays with baking paper.

2 Combine tahini, coriander, oil, seeds and salt in a large bowl. Tear kale into bite-size pieces. Using your hands, rub tahini mixture onto kale leaves to coat.

3 Place in a single layer on trays. Bake, swapping trays halfway through, for 50 minutes or until kale is dry and crisp.

KEEPS Store in an airtight container for up 2 weeks.

PEA, MISO AND MINT RICE PAPER ROLLS

PREP + COOK TIME **30 MINUTES** MAKES **10 ROLLS**

- 2 cups (240g) frozen peas, thawed
- 1 medium avocado (250g), chopped coarsely
- 1 tablespoon white (shiro) miso
- 1 teaspoon finely grated lime rind
- 1 tablespoon lime juice
- ¼ cup coarsely chopped fresh mint leaves

- 10 x 22cm (9-inch) rice papers rounds
- 2 cups (160g) finely shredded purple cabbage
- 2 cups julienned daikon
- 1 teaspoon black sesame seeds
- pickled ginger, to serve

1 Process peas, avocado, miso, lime rind, juice and mint until well combined but not quite smooth. Season to taste.

2 Place one rice paper round in a medium bowl of lukewarm water for 15 seconds or until just soft. Place on a clean tea towel or paper towel.

3 Place 1 tablespoon of the cabbage on the centre of each rice paper round, top with 2 tablespoons pea mixture; divide remaining cabbage and daikon among rice paper wrappers. Fold edges in and roll up firmly to enclose filling. Sprinkle with some black sesame seeds. Repeat with remaining rice paper rounds, filling and sesame seeds. Serve with pickled ginger.

KEEPS Best made on day of serving. Make a few hours ahead, then store, covered with damp paper towel in an airtight container in the fridge.

TIP You could sprinkle the chocolate-coated bars with desiccated coconut before refrigerating, if you like.

BOUNTIFUL BARS

PREP TIME **20 MINUTES (+ FREEZING & REFRIGERATION)** MAKES **16**

- 200g (6½ ounces) shredded coconut
- 2 tablespoons coconut oil, melted
- ½ cup (125ml) coconut cream
- ¼ teaspoon fine sea salt
- ¼ cup (90g) rice malt syrup

CACAO COATING
- ½ cup (100g) coconut oil
- ½ cup (120g) cacao butter, chopped finely
- ⅓ cup (80ml) pure maple syrup
- 1 cup (100g) cacao powder

1 Grease an 11cm x 21cm (4½-inch x 8½-inch), 1 litre (4-cup) loaf pan; line with plastic wrap, allowing excess to overhang sides. Line an oven tray with baking paper.
2 Process shredded coconut, coconut oil, coconut cream, salt and rice malt syrup until just combined. Firmly and evenly press mixture into loaf pan; freeze for 30 minutes or until firm.
3 Meanwhile, make cacao coating.
4 Remove coconut filling from freezer. Cut into eight bars; cut each bar in half horizontally. Using two forks, dip coconut bars in cacao coating until coated. Place on lined tray. Refrigerate for 30 minutes or until set. Trim off any excess chocolate.

CACAO COATING
Combine coconut oil, cacao butter and maple syrup in a heatproof bowl over a pan of boiling water; stir until melted and combined. Whisk in cacao powder until well combined.

KEEPS Store in an airtight container in the fridge for up to 2 weeks.

✳ This recipe is a perfect work lunch during cold and flu season; make a batch of the soup concentrate and keep in the freezer for when the cold weather hits. You will need four 2 cup (500ml) heatproof jars with lids for this recipe.

INSTANT FLU-HELPER CHICKEN NOODLE SOUP

PREP + COOK TIME **45 MINUTES (+ REFRIGERATION & FREEZING)** SERVES **4**

- 3 litres (12 cups) chicken broth (see page 61)
- 5cm (2-inch) piece fresh ginger, sliced thinly
- 5cm (2-inch) piece fresh turmeric, grated finely
- 2 cloves garlic, bruised
- 200g (6½ ounces) kelp noodles
- 1 cup (180g) frozen corn kernels, thawed
- 3 baby buk choy (450g), quartered lengthways
- 1 fresh long red chilli, sliced thinly, optional
- 1½ cups (220g) cooked chicken, sliced or shredded
- 6 green onions (scallions), sliced thinly
- 2 tablespoons tamari
- 1.5 litres (6 cups) boiling water

1 Combine chicken broth, ginger, turmeric and garlic in a large saucepan. Bring to the boil; boil for 35 minutes or until reduced to 3 cups (750ml). Strain through a fine sieve into a medium heatproof bowl; discard solids. Cool slightly; refrigerate for 2 hours.

2 Discard any solidified fat from broth surface. Pour broth concentrate into two ice cube trays; freeze for up to 3 months.

3 Divide noodles, corn, buk choy, chilli, chicken and green onion among four 2 cup (500ml) heatproof jars with lids. Add four frozen broth cubes and 2 teaspoons tamari to each jar.

4 Pour 1½ cups (375ml) of the boiling water into each jar; stir to dissolve broth cubes.

TIP To cook chicken
at the same time as
stock, gently simmer
a 250g (4-ounce)
chicken breast in
chicken stock (or
water) in a saucepan
over low heat for
10 minutes; cool in
stock for 5 minutes.
Cool and slice
thinly. Place in a
zip-top bag; freeze
for up to 1 month.

HONEY, MACADAMIA AND ROSEMARY SHORTBREAD

PREP + COOK TIME **45 MINUTES** MAKES **16 PIECES**

- 250g (8 ounces) unsalted butter, softened
- 2 tablespoons coconut sugar
- 2 tablespoons honey
- 2 cups (300g) white plain (all-purpose) spelt flour
- ⅓ cup (60g) rice flour
- 2 tablespoons finely chopped fresh rosemary
- ½ cup (75g) roasted macadamia halves, chopped coarsely

1 Preheat oven to 160°C/325°F. Line two oven trays with baking paper.

2 Beat butter and coconut sugar in a medium bowl with an electric mixer until light and fluffy. Beat in honey until well combined. Fold in sifted flours, rosemary and macadamias in two batches.

3 Divide dough in half, place each on a tray. Using lightly floured hands, press dough out to form 22cm (9-inch) rounds. Using fingertips, crimp edges to form a border. Using a sharp knife, score each shortbread into 8 wedges. Prick gently all over with a floured fork to create a pattern.

4 Bake, rotating trays halfway through, for 25 minutes or until golden. Cool on trays.

5 Using scored marks as a guide, cut into wedges.

SWAP OUT the macadamias for pine nuts or hazelnuts, if you like.

KEEPS Store in an airtight container for up to 2 weeks.

DILL PICKLE POPCORN

PREP + COOK TIME **10 MINUTES** MAKES **9 CUPS**

- 1 teaspoon ground coriander
- 1 teaspoon yellow mustard seeds
- 1 teaspoon black peppercorns
- 1 teaspoon garlic salt
- 1 teaspoon sea salt flakes
- ⅓ cup fresh dill sprigs, chopped finely
- ¼ cup (60ml) olive oil
- 2 tablespoons olive oil, extra
- ¾ cup (180g) popping corn

1 Crush spices and salts using a mortar and pestle. Stir in dill and oil.

2 Heat extra oil in a large heavy-based saucepan over medium heat. Add popping corn; cover and cook for 3 minutes, shaking pan occasionally or until all corn has popped.

3 Place popcorn in a large bowl; discard any unpopped kernels. Add dill seasoning; stir well to combine. Serve immediately.

VARIATIONS

NO-CHEESE CHEEZE

Omit ingredients in step 1. Combine ¼ cup (60ml) olive oil, 1 teaspoon smoked paprika, ½ teaspoon garlic salt and ¼ cup nutritional yeast flakes. Toss with hot popcorn.

WASABI, NORI AND SESAME

Omit ingredients in step 1. Snip two nori (seaweed) sheets into thin strips, using kitchen scissors. Combine 2 teaspoons each wasabi paste, tamari, sesame oil and olive oil until smooth. Toss wasabi mixture with hot popcorn. Add nori and 2 tablespoons sesame seeds; toss well to coat.

TIP Bee pollen, available from health food stores, is not for everyone; care should be taken for people with a history of reactions to grass and other airborne allergens.

CONFETTI BANANA AND TAHINI PUDDING

PREP TIME **5 MINUTES** SERVES **4**

- 3 medium ripe bananas (300g)
- 6 fresh dates (60g), pitted
- 1/3 cup (90g) hulled tahini
- 1/3 cup (80g) coconut oil, melted
- 2 tablespoons coconut milk
- 1 tablespoon pure vanilla extract
- 2 medium fresh figs (60g),
  cut into wedges

CONFETTI

- 2 tablespoons activated
  buckwheat groats
- 2 tablespoons pistachios,
  chopped coarsely
- 2 tablespoons shredded coconut
- 2 tablespoons cacao nibs
- 2 teaspoons black chia seeds
- 2 tablespoons dried rose petals,
  optional
- 1 tablepoon bee pollen (see tip),
  optional

1 Make confetti.

2 Blend banana, dates, tahini, coconut oil, coconut milk and vanilla until as smooth as possible, using a high-powered blender if available; this type of blender will produce a very smooth consistency.

3 Spoon evenly into four 3/4 cup (180ml) bowls. Top puddings with fig wedges; sprinkle with confetti.

CONFETTI

Combine all ingredients in a small bowl. (Makes about 1 cup)

TRY THIS

Sprinkle confetti over fruit smoothie bowls.

Stirred through coconut and vanilla ice-cream (see page 46), for added crunch.

SWAP OUT dried rose petals for 2 tablespoons pomegranate seeds and the bee pollen for a little fennel pollen, if you like, especially if you are concerned about bee or honey allergies.

KEEPS Pudding is best made just before serving. Store confetti in an airtight jar in the pantry for up to 2 weeks.

BERRYLICIOUS MOUSSE

PREP TIME **5 MINUTES (+ STANDING & REFRIGERATION)** SERVES **4**

If preferred, you can enjoy this immediately after making as a thick-style smoothie, rather than refrigerating to set.

- 1½ cup (225g) fresh or frozen raspberries
- ¾ cup (115g) fresh or frozen blueberries
- 300g (9½ ounces) silken tofu
- ¼ cup (90g) raw honey
- ½ teaspoon maqui powder (see tips), optional
- 1 tablespoon fresh or frozen raspberries, extra
- 1 tablespoon fresh or frozen blueberries, extra

1 If using frozen berries, thaw in a medium bowl at room temperature for 1 hour; drain.
2 Blend thawed berries, tofu, honey and maqui, if using, until as smooth as possible, using a high-powered blender if available; this type of blender will produce a very smooth consistency. Pour mixture evenly among four ¾ cup (180ml) glasses or jars.
3 Refrigerate for 4 hours or until firm. Top with extra berries before serving.

TRY THIS

Frozen in glasses, topped with frozen raspberries and blueberries, with raspberries on the stem, if you like (see opposite) for a refreshing fruit fix.
Layered with the coconut meringue mixture (see lemon meringue pie, page 173) in glasses for a parfait.
Topped with confetti (see confetti banana and tahini puddings, page 145).

KEEPS Cover with plastic wrap and store in the fridge for up to 4 days.

TIPS Maqui powder is available from some health food stores. It has a slightly sweet, tart flavour. Maqui berries are considered one of the highest antioxidant-rich fruits available.

TIPS You can use any leftover vegetable pulp from making fresh juice; we used carrot and beetroot. If you are making a fruit and vegetable juice, juice the vegetables first, then remove the pulp to use in the crackers before juicing the fruit. You can keep leftover pulp in the refrigerator for up to 2 days before making the crackers.

SEED AND VEGIE PULP CRISPBREADS

PREP + COOK TIME 4 HOURS 10 MINUTES (+ COOLING) MAKES 30

- ½ cup (80g) linseeds (flaxseeds)
- 2 tablespoons (20g) chia seeds
- ⅓ cup (80ml) water
- 1 tablespoon tamari
- 1 cup (150g) vegetable pulp, leftover from juicing (see tips)
- ¼ cup (35g) sunflower seeds
- 2 teaspoons sesame seeds
- ½ teaspoon cumin seeds
- 1 teaspoon caraway seeds
- 2 teaspoons raw honey

1 Preheat oven to 100°C/212°F. Lightly grease a 30cm x 40cm (12-inch x 16-inch) oven tray with baking paper.

2 Combine seeds, the water and tamari in a large bowl. Stand for 5 minutes. Add remaining ingredients; stir well to combine. Draw a 30cm x 40cm (12-inch x 16-inch) rectangle on a baking paper, turn it over. Spoon mixture onto centre of rectangle marked on baking paper; top with a second piece of paper. Roll mixture out to fill rectangle, remove top paper; transfer to oven tray on baking paper. If you prefer even-sized crackers, score mixture with a sharp knife into 5cm (2-inch) squares.

3 Bake for 2 hours, turn cracker over and bake for a further 2 hours or until dried and crisp. Turn oven off; leave cracker inside to cool completely.

4 Break cooled cracker into pieces; alternatively, using score lines, break into squares. Transfer to an airtight container.

<u>TRY THESE</u>
With a bowl of loads-in-one goodness smash (see page 70), for dipping.
Spread with cashew cream cheese (see page 158).
Dunked in 15-minute herby pea and coconut soup (see page 154).

<u>KEEPS</u> Store crackers in an airtight container for up to 4 days.

RAW SLAW SALAD WITH PUMPERNICKEL CRUMBS

PREP TIME **15 MINUTES** SERVES **2**

Serves two as a vegetarian main or serve as a side dish for four with grilled salmon or pork.

- 125g (4 ounces) brussels sprouts
- 1 baby cauliflower (125g)
- 1 small fennel bulb (200g)
- ¼ cup (40g) sultanas
- 1½ teaspoon apple cider vinegar
- ⅓ cup (80ml) extra virgin olive oil
- ½ teaspoon sea salt flakes
- ½ teaspoon cracked black pepper
- ¼ cup (70g) Greek-style yoghurt
- 1 slice pumpernickel rye bread (50g), chopped coarsely
- 1 teaspoon capers
- ½ medium green apple (75g)

1 Trim base and outer leaves from sprouts. Using a sharp knife, thinly slice sprouts and cauliflower; place in a large bowl. Trim fennel; reserve half of the fronds. Thinly slice fennel; add to bowl.

2 Combine sultanas, vinegar, ¼ cup of the oil, salt, pepper and yoghurt in a small bowl.

3 Process pumpernickel until large breadcrumbs form. Heat a medium frying pan over high heat. Add crumbs to dry pan; cook, stirring continuously, for 4 minutes or until toasted.

4 Heat the remaining oil in a small frying pan over high heat; add capers. Cook, stirring for 2 minutes or until capers have burst their skins. (Be careful as the capers will pop in the hot oil and may splash.)

5 Cut apple lengthways into thin slices. Add to vegetable mixture. Pour over yoghurt dressing; mix gently to combine.

6 Serve salad sprinkled with toasted crumbs, capers and reserved fennel fronds.

PEANUT BUTTER AND BEETROOT HUMMUS

PREP TIME 10 MINUTES SERVES 8 (MAKES 3 CUPS)

- 3 medium beetroot (500g)
- ¼ cup (60ml) lemon juice
- ½ cup (130g) natural crunchy peanut butter
- 1 cup (200g) cannellini beans
- 1 teaspoon sea salt flakes
- 2 cloves garlic, peeled
- ¼ teaspoon ground cumin
- ½ cup fresh coriander (cilantro) leaves

PITTA BREAD CRISPS

- 2 large wholemeal lebanese bread rounds (200g)
- 2 tablespoons extra virgin olive oil
- 1 teaspoon ground cumin
- 1 teaspoon sumac
- ¼ teaspoon sea salt flakes

1 Make pitta bread crisps.
2 Wearing kitchen gloves, peel beetroot, then chop coarsely.
3 Process beetroot with remaining ingredients until smooth.
4 Serve dip with pitta crisps.

PITTA BREAD CRISPS

Preheat oven to 200°C/400°F. Using scissors, snip around edge of bread rounds, then pull apart to separate. Place crumb-side up on two large oven trays. Brush with oil; sprinkle with spices. Bake, swapping trays from top to bottom, for 4 minutes or until golden. Cool; season lightly with salt. Break into large pieces.

KEEPS Store dip in the fridge for up to 3 days. The pitta bread crisps will keep in an airtight container in the pantry for up to 1 week.

SWAP OUT the peanut butter with the same quantity of almond or macadamia spread, if preferred.

SERVE WITH halved or quartered baby cucumbers.

15-MINUTE HERBY PEA AND COCONUT SOUP

PREP + COOK TIME **15 MINUTES** SERVES **6**

- 2 tablespoons coconut oil
- 200g (7 ounces) green onions (scallions), sliced
- 1kg (2 pounds) frozen peas
- 400ml can coconut cream
- 3 teaspoons sea salt flakes, or to taste
- 3 cups (750ml) boiling water

- ⅓ cup (80ml) lemon juice
- 2 cups fresh basil leaves
- 2 cups fresh coriander (cilantro) leaves
- ½ cup fresh dill sprigs
- ½ cup fresh mint sprigs
- Greek-style yoghurt or unsweetened coconut yoghurt, to serve, optional

1 Heat coconut oil in a large saucepan over medium-high heat. Cook onion, stirring for 3 minutes or until softened. Increase heat to high; add peas, coconut cream, salt and the water. Bring to the boil; cook, stirring occasionally, for 5 minutes or until peas are heated through.

2 Remove from heat, add lemon juice and all but ½ cup of the combined herbs. Cool for 5 minutes; process in batches until smooth. Return soup to pan; heat briefly until just warmed through.

3 Serve soup in bowls topped with remaining herbs and yoghurt, if you like; season to taste.

RAW CHOC CHIP COOKIE DOUGH

PREP TIME 15 MINUTES (+ REFRIGERATION) SERVES 8

- 100g (3 ounces) brazil nuts
- 200g (6½ ounces) natural almonds
- 1 vanilla bean
- ¼ cup (60ml) pure maple syrup
- ¼ teaspoon ground cinnamon
- 2 tablespoons coconut oil, at room temperature
- 1 teaspoon sea salt flakes
- ¼ cup (30g) cacao nibs

1 Line an 18cm x 28cm (7¼-inch x 11¼-inch) oven tray with baking paper.

2 Process nuts until fine crumbs form. Split vanilla bean lengthways; scrape seeds from halves, using the tip of a knife. Add seeds to processor with syrup, cinnamon, coconut oil and salt. Pulse until a soft dough forms; it will be quite sticky.

3 Press dough into lined oven tray, using a spoon dipped in a little cold water. Sprinkle over 2 tablespoons of the cacao nibs; press into dough. Refrigerate for 25 minutes or until firm.

4 Lift baking paper and dough from tray. Using paper as an aid, roll dough into a sausage shape. Sprinkle over remaining cacao nibs, reroll in paper, then in foil. Twist ends of foil and paper to form a tight log. Refrigerate for a further 20 minutes or until firm.

5 Cut into thick slices; serve.

KEEPS Store raw cookie dough in a container in the fridge for up to 5 days.

SERVE WITH coconut and vanilla ice-cream (see page 46) and chopped sugar-free chocolate, if you like.

CHEAT'S TEFF FLATBREAD WITH CASHEW CREAM CHEESE

PREP + COOK TIME **50 MINUTES (+ STANDING)** SERVES **4**

You will need to start this recipe a day ahead.
It's gluten-free and dairy-free.

- ⅔ cup (100g) teff flour (see tips)
- 1 teaspoon gluten-free baking powder
- ¼ teaspoon sea salt flakes
- 1 teaspoon nigella seeds
- ⅓ cup (80ml) water
- 3 eggs
- 1 teaspoon apple cider vinegar
- 1 teaspoon coconut oil or cooking oil spray

CASHEW CREAM CHEESE

- 1⅔ cups (250g) raw cashews
- 2 teaspoons sea salt flakes
- 2 teaspoons nutritional yeast flakes (see page 236)
- 3 teaspoons olive oil
- ⅓ cup (80ml) water
- 2 tablespoons lemon juice
- 1 clove garlic

1 Make cashew cream cheese.
2 Sift flour and baking powder into a medium bowl; stir in salt and seeds. Make a well in the centre; whisk in water, eggs and vinegar.
3 Heat a 20cm (8-inch) wide, 15cm (6-inch) base non-stick frying pan over medium heat. Brush pan with ¼ teaspoon of the coconut oil or coat lightly with oil spray. Pour ⅓ cup of the batter into hot pan; spread with an offset palette knife to cover pan. Cook for 2 minutes each side or until cooked through. Transfer flatbread to a plate; cover to keep warm.
4 Repeat with remaining batter to make four flatbreads. Cut into wedges; serve topped with cashew cream cheese.

CASHEW CREAM CHEESE

Place cashews in a small bowl; cover with cold water. Stand, covered, for 4 hours or overnight. Drain cashews; rinse under cold water, drain well. Blend nuts with remaining ingredients, using a high-powered blender if available; this type of blender will produce a very smooth consistency. (Makes 2 cups)

KEEPS Flatbreads are best made on day of serving or can be frozen for up to 1 month. Store cashew cream cheese in an airtight container in the fridge for up to 3 weeks.

TRY THIS topped with halved or quartered mixed heirloom cherry tomatoes and small basil leaves, seasoned with salt and pepper.

TIPS Teff flour is derived from the seeds of a hardy grass. It is a staple in Ethiopia, where it is used to make injera, a fermented flatbread. Teff is high in protein, calcium and resistant starch, a form of dietary fibre that can help with blood-sugar management. The pleasant nutty taste and its gluten-free status have contributed to its popularity in western countries. Teff flour is available from some supermarkets, delis and health food stores.

TIPS While the nuts are roasting, start step 3, so that the nuts are warm when you toss them with the syrup. You will need to work rapidly, as the syrup sets quickly. Always take care around hot syrups as they can cause nasty burns.

POWDERED PECANS AND ALMONDS WITH ROSEMARY

PREP + COOK TIME **25 MINUTES (+ COOLING)** MAKES **4½ CUPS**

- 2 cups (240g) pecans
- 2 cups (320g) natural almonds
- 1 tablespoon finely chopped fresh rosemary
- 1 teaspoon sea salt flakes
- ½ teaspoon freshly ground black pepper
- ¾ cup (180ml) rice malt syrup

1 Preheat oven to 180°C/350°F.

2 Place nuts on an oven tray; roast for 10 minutes or until light golden (see tips). Transfer immediately to a large heatproof bowl. Add rosemary, salt and pepper; toss to combine.

3 Meanwhile, place rice malt syrup in a small heavy-based saucepan over high heat. Cook without stirring, swirling pan occasionally, for 10 minutes or until syrup reaches 150°C/300°F (hard crack stage) on a sugar (candy) thermometer. (Alternatively, drop a spoonful of syrup into a glass of ice-cold water; syrup should form brittle threads that will break when bent.)

4 Working quickly, add syrup to warm nut mixture; stir vigorously (see tips) with a metal spoon until syrup hardens and nuts are cool enough to handle. Using your hands, roughly break up and toss nuts together, roughing up surface.

5 Leave nuts to cool completely; transfer to a large airtight jar.

KEEPS Store nuts in the pantry for up to 2 weeks.

RAW LAMINGTONS

PREP TIME 1 HOUR (+ STANDING & FREEZING) MAKES 17

You will need to start this recipe a day ahead.

- 1⅓ cups (200g) raw cashews
- 150g cacao butter, chopped
- ⅔ cup (70g) cacao powder
- ½ cup (180g) raw honey
- ½ cup (40g) shredded coconut
- 1 cup (240g) coconut oil
- ¼ teaspoon pure vanilla extract
- 2 teaspoons rice malt syrup
- 1 cup (75g) shredded coconut, extra

RASPBERRY CHIA JAM

- 1½ cups (225g) frozen raspberries
- 2 tablespoons warm tap water
- 2 tablespoons raw honey
- 2 tablespoons white chia seeds

1 Place cashews in a medium bowl; cover with cold water. Stand, covered, for 4 hours or overnight. Drain cashews, rinse under cold water; drain well.

2 Make raspberry chia jam.

3 Grease a 20cm x 30cm (8-inch x 12-inch) slice pan; line with baking paper.

4 Place cacao butter in a small heavy-based saucepan over medium heat; stir until melted. Add cacao powder and half the honey; stir until smooth. Remove from heat; stir through shredded coconut. Spread mixture evenly into pan; freeze for 30 minutes or until set.

5 Place coconut oil, vanilla and remaining honey in a clean small heavy-based saucepan; stir over medium heat for 5 minutes or until melted and combined. Blend coconut oil mixture with soaked cashews, using a high-powered blender if available; this type of blender will produce a very smooth consistency. Cool and spread evenly over chilled cocoa layer, using a spatula. Cover with plastic wrap; freeze for 2 hours or until set.

6 Using a hot, dry knife, cut into 4cm (1½-inch) squares. Place 1 teaspoon jam on half of the squares; top with remaining squares to sandwich. Brush tops with rice malt syrup; sprinkle with extra shredded coconut. Transfer to an airtight container; freeze until required.

RASPBERRY CHIA JAM

Place raspberries in a food processor bowl or blender; stand until thawed. Stir warmed tap water (no hotter than 60°C/140°F) and honey in a small bowl to loosen; add to raspberries. Blend or process until pureed, transfer to a small bowl; stir in chia seeds. Cover and refrigerate for at least 3 hours or overnight until thickened to a jam-like consistency.

KEEPS Store leftover jam in a jar in the fridge for up to 3 days. Store raw lamingtons in an airtight container in the freezer for up 2 weeks.

TIPS Spread leftover
jam over toast or
swirl through your
favourite yoghurt.
Try replacing
raspberries with
the same amount of
fresh strawberries.

BLACKBERRY, APPLE AND ALMOND BRAN MUFFINS

PREP + COOK TIME **1 HOUR (+ REFRIGERATION)** MAKES **12**

You will need to start the coconut whip recipe
a day ahead.

- 1½ cups (225g) plain (all-purpose) flour
- 1 cup (120g) oat bran
- 2 teaspoons baking powder
- 1 teaspoon bicarbonate of soda (baking soda)
- ¼ teaspoon salt
- 1 cup (170g) coarsely grated apple (see tip)
- 1 cup (150g) frozen blackberries

- 2 eggs
- 2 tablespoons raw honey
- 1¼ cup (310ml) almond milk
- ⅓ cup (95g) almond spread
- 1 teaspoon pure vanilla extract
- 1 teaspoon oat bran, extra
- ½ cup (40g) flaked almonds, roasted

COCONUT-BLACKBERRY WHIP

- 270ml can coconut cream, unopened
- 2 tablespoons raw honey
- ⅓ cup (50g) frozen blackberries, thawed, patted dry

1 Make coconut-blackberry whip.

2 Preheat oven 180°C/350°F. Grease two 6-hole (¾ cup/180ml) texas muffin pans; line with large squares of baking paper.

3 Place flour, bran, baking powder, bicarbonate of soda and salt in a large bowl; whisk to combine. Fold in apple and half the berries.

4 Whisk eggs, honey, milk, almond spread and vanilla in a medium bowl. Pour over dry ingredients; fold until almost combined.

5 Spoon mixture into muffin holes, sprinkle with extra bran and push remaining berries into tops of muffins.

6 Bake for 20 minutes or until a skewer inserted into the centre of a middle muffin comes out clean. Cool in pans.

7 Dollop coconut-blackberry whip on cooled muffins; top with almonds.

COCONUT-BLACKBERRY WHIP

Chill coconut cream can overnight in the fridge, so that the cream separates and sets on top. Without shaking or tipping the can, carefully spoon out thick cream on top. Beat coconut cream, honey and berries with an electric mixer on high speed for 5 minutes until thickened slightly. Refrigerate.

TIP You will need 2 medium apples for the amount of grated apple in recipe.

✱ Try this mix as a post-work out snack, or keep a jar handy on your desk at work for times when you might crave a sugary treat. A handful of the mix will help stabilise blood sugars until a proper meal can be had.

SPICY KEEP·ON·GOING MIX

PREP + COOK TIME **20 MINUTES** MAKES **3 CUPS**

- 1½ tablespoons raw honey
- ½ teaspoon cayenne pepper
- ½ teaspoon smoked paprika
- 1½ teaspoons fine sea salt
- 1½ tablespoons coconut oil
- 1 cup (160g) natural almonds
- ½ cup (70g) skinless hazelnuts
- ½ cup (100g) pepitas (pumpkin seed kernels)
- ¼ cup (35g) sunflower seeds
- ½ cup (25g) flaked coconut

1 Preheat oven to 150°C/300°F. Line a large oven tray with baking paper.

2 Combine honey, spices, salt and coconut oil in a large bowl. Add nuts, seeds and coconut; mix until well coated.

3 Spread mixture out in a single layer on tray.

4 Bake, stirring occasionally, for 15 minutes or until lightly browned. Cool on tray. Separate into small clusters.

KEEPS Store in an airtight container for up to 1 week.

SWEET
STUFF

KEY LIME TARTLETS

PREP TIME **25 MINUTES (+ STANDING & REFRIGERATION)** MAKES **12**

- 1½ cups (225g) cashews
- ⅔ cup (150g) fresh dates, pitted, chopped coarsely
- 1½ cups (115g) shredded coconut, toasted
- ½ teaspoon sea salt flakes
- ⅔ cup (150g) coconut oil, melted
- ½ cup (125ml) lime juice
- ¼ cup (60ml) lemon juice
- 2 avocados (500g), chopped coarsely
- ⅓ cup (80ml) pure maple syrup
- 8 drops stevia
- thinly sliced lime rind, to serve

1 Place cashews in a small bowl; cover with cold water. Stand, covered, for 2 hours. Drain cashews, rinse under cold water; drain well.

2 Process one-third of cashews until finely chopped. Add dates and process to form an almost smooth paste. Add shredded coconut, half of the salt and 2 tablespoons of the coconut oil; pulse to combine.

3 Line a 12-hole (⅓ cup/80ml) muffin tin with 2 strips of baking paper in a cross, over base and up sides of pan. Press slightly heaped tablespoons of the mixture into each case, firmly pressing up against sides. Refrigerate until needed.

4 Blend remaining cashews with remaining ingredients, using a high-powered blender, if available; this type of blender will produce a very smooth consistency. Spoon mixture evenly into cases; refrigerate for at least 4 hours or until set. Serve topped with lime rind.

KEEPS Store in an airtight container in the fridge for up to 4 days.

TIPS Use the
reserved coconut
water in your next
smoothie. The pie
can also be made
in a 24cm (9½ inch)
tart tin.

LEMON MERINGUE PIE

PREP TIME **45 MINUTES (+ STANDING & FREEZING)** SERVES **12**

You will need to start this recipe a day ahead.

- 2 cups (300g) raw cashews
- 1½ cups (255g) activated buckwheat groats
- 1½ cups (180g) pecans
- 8 fresh dates (160g), pitted
- ⅓ cup (70g) coconut oil, melted
- ½ cup (125ml) coconut cream
- ¼ cup (90g) raw honey
- 2 tablespoons finely grated lemon rind
- ½ cup (125ml) lemon juice
- ¾ teaspoon ground turmeric
- ½ cup (100g) coconut oil, melted, extra

COCONUT MERINGUES

- 3 young drinking coconuts (3.6kg)
- ½ cup (125ml) coconut cream
- 1½ tablespoons raw honey
- ⅓ cup (70g) coconut oil, melted
- 1 teaspoon lemon juice

1 Place cashews in a medium bowl; cover with cold water. Stand, covered, for 4 hours or overnight. Drain cashews; rinse under cold water, drain well.

2 Grease a 25cm (10-inch), 3cm (1¼-inch) deep loose-based tart tin.

3 Process buckwheat, pecans, dates and coconut oil until mixture resembles coarse crumbs and holds together when pressed. Press mixture firmly and evenly over base and up side of tin to form a crust, using the back of a spoon. Freeze for 4 hours or overnight.

4 Blend drained cashews, coconut cream, honey, rind, juice and turmeric until smooth. Add extra coconut oil and blend until as smooth as possible, using a high-powered blender, if available; this type of blender will produce a very smooth consistency. Spread lemon filling over tart base; smooth top. Freeze for 4 hours or until firm.

5 Meanwhile, make coconut meringues.

6 Spoon meringue mixture into a piping bag fitted with a 1.5cm (¾-inch) plain tube; pipe rounds on top of pie, creating small peaks (teardrops). Freeze pie for 2 hours or until meringues are firm. (Meringues will not set as firmly as the filling.)

COCONUT MERINGUES

Place a coconut on its side on a chopping board; carefully cut off the dome-shaped top with a cleaver or large knife. You will need a large enough hole to be able to scoop out the flesh with a spoon — you will also need to use a bit of force. Drain coconut water into a large jug (reserve for another use, see tips). Spoon out the soft flesh. Repeat with remaining coconuts; you should have about 3 cups (270g) of the flesh. Blend flesh with remaining ingredients until as smooth as possible, using a high-powered blender, if available; this type of blender will produce a very smooth consistency. Pour meringue mixture into a small bowl. Cover; freeze for 2 hours or until thick. Whisk mixture vigorously to achieve an even consistency. Transfer to a medium bowl; refrigerate to firm while lemon filling sets.

KEEPS Store pie in an airtight container in the fridge for up to 5 days or freeze, without meringues, for up to 2 months.

✳ These dairy and gluten-free doughnuts are superfast
to make, however, you will need a special doughnut-shaped
pan, available from kitchenware stores, for this recipe.

PEACHES AND CREAM DOUGHNUTS

PREP + COOK TIME **30 MINUTES (+ STANDING)** MAKES **6**

- ½ cup (120g) drained canned peach slices in natural juice (see tips)
- ¼ cup (60ml) coconut cream
- 1 egg
- 1 teaspoon pure vanilla extract
- 1½ cups (180g) almond meal
- 2 tablespoons stevia powder
- 1 teaspoon baking powder
- ⅓ cup (50g) dried peaches, chopped finely
- 2 tablespoons finely chopped pecans
- 1 tablespoon dried cornflower petals, optional

PEACH GLAZE

- ½ cup (125ml) canned peach juice (see tips)
- ½ cup (50g) coconut milk powder
- 1 teaspoon cornflour (cornstarch)
- ½ teaspoon pure vanilla extract

1 Preheat oven to 180°C/350°F. Grease a 6-hole (⅓ cup/80ml) non-stick doughnut pan.

2 Blend or process peaches, coconut cream, egg and vanilla until smooth. Add almond meal, stevia and baking powder; blend or process to combine. Spoon evenly into pan.

3 Bake for 20 minutes or until a skewer inserted into the centre of a doughnut comes out clean. Stand doughnuts in pan for 5 minutes. Turn, top-side up, onto a wire rack over a tray.

4 Make peach glaze.

5 Dip doughnuts in warm glaze; sprinkle with dried peach, pecans and cornflower petals, if using. Cool on a wire rack.

PEACH GLAZE

Place all ingredients in a small heavy-based saucepan; whisk well until smooth. Bring to a simmer over high heat, whisking continuously until thick.

SWAP OUT peach slices in natural juice for plum slices and juice and almond meal for hazelnut meal. Omit dried peaches and sprinkle with freeze-dried rose petals and finely chopped unsalted pistachios.

TIPS You will need a 400g (12½-ounce) can of peach slices in natural juices; reserve ½ cup drained fruit for the doughnuts and ¼ cup of the drained syrup for the glaze. Some brands of vanilla extract contain a negligible amount of added sucrose. Edible dried cornflower petals are available from some gourmet food stores and online.

TIPS Ensure that the gelatine mixture has cooled before combining it with the kombucha or the excess heat will destroy the probiotics in the kombucha. To make this ice-cream without an ice-cream machine, pour the cashew mixture into a large zip-top plastic bag; seal. Freeze, flat-side down, on a large tray for 1 hour or until partially frozen. Process mixture until smooth. Repeat freezing and processing mixture once more. Spoon into the loaf pan and freeze for 2 hours or until the consistency of soft-serve ice-cream.

KOMBUCHA BERRY JELLIES WITH CINNAMON-CASHEW ICE-CREAM

PREP + COOK TIME **35 MINUTES (+ STANDING, REFRIGERATION & FREEZING)** SERVES **4**

You will need to start this recipe a day ahead.

- 1 cup (250ml) apple juice
- 2cm (¾-inch) piece ginger (10g), sliced thinly
- 4 teaspoons (14g) powdered gelatine
- 2 cups (500ml) hibiscus-flavoured kombucha
- 125g (4 ounces) fresh raspberries
- 125g (4 ounces) fresh blueberries, halved if large

CINNAMON-CASHEW ICE-CREAM

- 1½ cups (225g) raw cashews
- 1¼ cups (310ml) water
- 2 tablespoons pure maple syrup
- 1 teaspoon vanilla bean paste
- ½ teaspoon ground cinnamon
- ¼ teaspoon fine sea salt

1 Heat juice and ginger in a small saucepan over medium heat until mixture is just simmering. Remove from heat; quickly sprinkle over gelatine; whisk to dissolve. Pour into a large bowl; cool to room temperature.

2 Discard ginger slices. Add kombucha to juice mixture (see tips); whisk to combine. Stand for 5 minutes to allow any bubbles to settle.

3 Divide three-quarters of the berries among four 1-cup (250ml) bundt or jelly moulds. Pour in jelly mixture; refrigerate for 4 hours or overnight until set.

4 Make cinnamon cashew ice-cream.

5 Dip moulds in boiling water briefly to release jellies. Turn out onto serving plates. Serve topped with scoops of cinnamon-cashew ice-cream and remaining berries.

CINNAMON-CASHEW ICE-CREAM

Place cashews in a large bowl; cover with cold water. Stand, covered, for at least 2 hours or overnight. Drain cashews, rinse under cold water; drain well. Blend cashews with remaining ingredients until as smooth as possible, using a high-powered blender, if available; this type of blender will produce a very smooth consistency. Churn mixture in an ice-cream maker, following manufacturer's instructions, until the consistency of soft-serve ice-cream. Spoon into a 3-cup (750ml) loaf pan; cover and freeze for 2 hours. Remove from freezer 15 minutes before serving.

Our generous, dreamily rich slice with crunchy little pockets of nuts and buckwheat is inspired by beloved Ferrero Rocher chocolates.

CHOCOLATE HAZELNUT SLICE

PREP TIME **50 MINUTES** (+ STANDING, FREEZING & REFRIGERATION) MAKES **16**

You will need to start this recipe a day ahead.

- 2 cups (300g) raw cashews
- 2 cups (280g) hazelnuts
- ½ cup (60g) almond meal
- ⅓ cup (35g) cacao powder
- 2 teaspoons pure vanilla extract
- ¾ cup (150g) activated buckwheat groats (see tips)
- ⅓ cup (80ml) coconut nectar
- ⅔ cup (140g) coconut oil, melted
- ½ cup (140g) chocolate hazelnut spread
- ½ cup (125ml) pure maple syrup
- ¼ cup (60ml) coconut cream
- ⅛ teaspoon natural hazelnut flavour (see tips)
- ¼ teaspoon fine sea salt

CHOCOLATE GANACHE

- ¾ cup (75g) cacao powder
- ⅓ cup (70g) coconut oil, melted
- ¾ cup (180ml) pure maple syrup
- ½ teaspoon pure vanilla extract

1 Place cashews in a large bowl; cover with cold water. Stand, covered, for 4 hours or overnight. Drain cashews, rinse under cold water; drain well.

2 Lightly grease or oil an 18cm x 28cm (7¼-inch x 11¼-inch) slice pan; line base and sides with baking paper, extending the paper 5cm (2 inches) over sides.

3 Process 1 cup of the hazelnuts, the almond meal, cacao powder and half the vanilla until mixture resembles coarse crumbs. Add buckwheat groats, nectar and 2 tablespoons of the coconut oil; process until just combined. Press nut mixture firmly and evenly over base of pan, using a plastic spatula. Freeze while preparing filling.

4 Blend drained cashews with remaining coconut oil, chocolate hazelnut spread, syrup, coconut cream, remaining vanilla, hazelnut flavour and salt until as smooth as possible, using a high-powered blender, if available; this type of blender will produce a very smooth consistency. Pour half the mixture over base; smooth top.

5 Finely chop ⅔ cup of the remaining hazelnuts; sprinkle over filling. Pour over remaining cashew mixture; smooth top. Cover; freeze for 3 hours or until firm.

6 Make chocolate ganache.

7 Pour chocolate ganache over slice; smooth top. Refrigerate for 20 minutes.

8 Coarsely chop remaining hazelnuts. Sprinkle over slice.

9 Cut slice into rectangles.

CHOCOLATE GANACHE

Blend ingredients until as smooth as possible, using a high-powered blender, if available; this type of blender will produce a very smooth consistency.

KEEPS Store in an airtight container in the fridge for up to 6 days or freezer for up to 2 months.

TIPS Activated
buckwheat groats are
available from health
food stores; they add
a delicious crunch.
Natural hazelnut
flavour is available
from selected health
food stores or can
be purchased online.
Hazelnut flavour may
vary depending on
the brand. We used
Medicine Flower's
natural hazelnut
flavour. If using
hazelnut oil or
hazelnut essence,
use only 1 or 2 drops;
for hazelnut extract
use about ½ teaspoon.

CHOCOLATE CARAMEL GOOD TIMES

PREP + COOK TIME **30 MINUTES (+ STANDING & FREEZING)** MAKES **12**

You will need to start this recipe 2 days ahead.

- 2 cups (300g) raw cashews
- 1 cup (250ml) coconut cream
- 2 tablespoons coconut oil, melted
- ¼ cup (60ml) pure maple syrup
- 1 cup (140g) slivered almonds, roasted, chopped coarsely

CARAMEL SAUCE

- 1 cup (250ml) coconut cream
- ⅓ cup (80ml) pure maple syrup
- 1 vanilla bean, split lengthways, seeds scraped

CHOCOLATE COATING

- 75g (2½ ounces) cacao butter, chopped finely
- 2 tablespoons pure maple syrup
- ½ cup (50g) cacao powder

1 Place cashews in a small bowl; cover with cold water. Stand, covered, for 4 hours or overnight.
2 Meanwhile, make caramel sauce.
3 Drain cashews, rinse under cold water; drain well. Blend cashews with coconut cream, coconut oil and syrup, using a high-powered blender if available; this type of blender will produce a very smooth consistency.
4 Dollop cashew and caramel mixtures alternately in each hole of two 6-hole (⅓ cup/80ml) popsicle moulds. Push a popsicle stick into each mould; freeze overnight or until firm.
5 When ready to coat the frozen popsicles, make chocolate coating.
6 Line an oven tray with baking paper; place in the freezer. Pour chocolate coating into a small jug. Place almonds in a small bowl. Dip popsicle mould briefly in hot water; remove popsicles. Dip popsicles into chocolate coating; dip in almonds to coat evenly.
7 Place on chilled tray. Freeze for 5 minutes or until coating is set.

CARAMEL SAUCE
Place all ingredients in a small saucepan. Bring to the boil over medium heat, reduce heat to low; simmer, stirring occasionally, for 25 minutes or until thickened. Remove vanilla. Transfer to a small bowl, cover with plastic wrap; refrigerate until chilled. (Makes about ¾ cup)

CHOCOLATE COATING
Place cacao butter in a medium heatproof bowl over a smaller heatproof bowl of boiling water, whisk until combined and smooth; whisk in syrup. Whisk in cacao powder until combined and smooth. Cool to room temperature.

TROPICAL CHOC-DIPPED FRUIT

PREP TIME **40 MINUTES (+ REFRIGERATION)** SERVES **10**

You will need to visit a good health or gourmet food store to gather the unique ingredients for this recipe – that's the hard part. Making your own chocolate, dipping the fruit and coating it are the easy bits, resulting in a spectacular dessert.

- 1kg (2-pound) piece watermelon, cut into small wedges
- 1 medium mandarin (200g), segmented
- 1 cup (150g) cherries
- 1 cup (130g) strawberries
- 1 medium kiwifruit (85g), sliced
- 8 purchased dehydrated orange slices (see tips)
- 8 purchased dehydrated pineapple slices (see tips)

CRUNCHY ADD-ONS

- 2 tablespoons freeze-dried raspberries, crushed
- 1 tablespoon desiccated coconut
- 1 tablespoon slivered pistachios, chopped
- 1 tablespoon unsprayed dried salad flowers (see tips)
- 1 tablespoon unsprayed freeze-dried rose petals
- 1 tablespoon activated buckwheat groats
- 2 teaspoons freeze-dried raspberry powder
- 1 teaspoon bee pollen, optional (see page 42)

CHOCOLATE COATING

- 2 tablespoons coconut oil
- ½ cup (120g) cacao butter, chopped finely
- 2 tablespoons pure maple syrup
- ½ teaspoon pure vanilla extract
- ¾ cup (100g) cacao powder

1 Place fruit on trays lined with baking paper. With a paper towel, pat watermelon dry to remove excess moisture.

2 Place crunchy add-ons in separate small bowls.

3 Make chocolate coating.

4 Working in batches, beginning with the smaller fruits, dip fruit into chocolate coating; allow excess chocolate to drain off. Sprinkle with a selection of crunchy add-ons; place on tray. If chocolate starts to thicken, reheat. Refrigerate choc-dipped fruit for 15 minutes or until chocolate is set.

5 Pour any leftover chocolate coating onto a plate lined with baking paper; sprinkle with leftover crunchy add-ons. Refrigerate for 15 minutes or until chocolate is set. Break into pieces and serve with the choc-dipped fruit.

CHOCOLATE COATING

Place coconut oil and cacao butter in a medium heatproof bowl over a smaller heatproof bowl of boiling water; whisk until combined and smooth. Whisk in syrup and vanilla; remove from heat. Whisk in cacao until combined and smooth.

TIPS You can use any combination of fresh, dried and dehydrated fruit. Dried salad flowers are available from The Essential Ingredient, labelled 'Salade de Fleur'.

RAW CARROT CAKE WITH COCONUT 'CREAM CHEESE' FROSTING

PREP TIME 35 MINUTES (+ REFRIGERATION & STANDING) SERVES 12

You will need to start this recipe a day ahead.

- 225ml can coconut cream, unopened
- 1 cup (150g) raw cashews
- 1 cup (120g) almond meal
- ½ teaspoon ground nutmeg
- 2 teaspoons ground cinnamon
- 1 teaspoon ground ginger
- 1⅓ cups (285g) coarsely chopped fresh pitted dates
- ¼ teaspoon fine sea salt
- 6 carrots (720g), peeled, grated finely
- 1 cup (80g) desiccated coconut
- ⅓ cup (55g) sultanas
- 1¼ cups (125g) walnuts, chopped coarsely
- ¼ cup (60ml) pure maple syrup
- 2 tablespoons coconut oil, melted
- 1 vanilla bean, split lengthways, seeds scraped

1 Chill coconut cream can overnight in the fridge, so that the cream separates and sets on top.

2 Place cashews in a small bowl; cover with cold water. Stand, covered for 4 hours or overnight. Drain cashews, rinse under cold water; drain well.

3 Grease a 20cm (8-inch) springform cake pan; line base and side with baking paper.

4 Process almond meal, spices, dates and half of the salt until finely chopped and mixture sticks together.

5 Squeeze out all excess liquid from carrot. Add carrot and coconut to food processor; pulse until combined. Remove blade from processor; stir in sultanas and two-thirds of the walnuts until combined. Transfer mixture to lined cake pan; press down firmly on it to ensure it is packed in well. Refrigerate for at least 1 hour.

6 Meanwhile, to make coconut 'cream cheese' frosting, without shaking or tipping coconut cream can, carefully spoon out thickened coconut cream into a small bowl of an electric mixer (reserve thin liquid in an airtight container in the fridge for another use). Beat coconut cream with an electric mixer for 5 minutes or until soft peaks form.

7 Blend soaked cashews, syrup, coconut oil, vanilla seeds and remaining salt until very smooth, using a high-powered blender, if available; this type of blender will produce a very smooth consistency. Fold cashew mixture into whipped coconut cream in a bowl until combined. Cover bowl with plastic wrap; refrigerate for 20 minutes or until it is a spreadable consistency.

8 Release cake from pan, transfer to a plate; spread with frosting. Refrigerate for a further 30 minutes until firm. Top with remaining walnuts to serve.

SWAP OUT the walnuts for pecans and almond meal for hazelnut meal.

TRY THIS topped with baby (dutch) carrots halved lengthways and drizzled with pure maple syrup, if you like.

COCONUT STICKY RICE ICE-CREAM WITH MANGO

PREP + COOK TIME **1 HOUR 30 MINUTES (+ STANDING, COOLING, REFRIGERATION & FREEZING)** SERVES **4**

You will need to start this recipe a day ahead.

- 75g (2½ ounces) black glutinous rice
- 1 pandan leaf, tied in a knot, optional
- 2 cups (500ml) water
- 2 x 400ml cans coconut cream
- ¾ cup (275g) rice malt syrup
- ¼ cup (60g) coconut oil
- ¾ teaspoon sea salt
- 2 tablespoons arrowroot
- 2 tablespoons black sesame seeds
- 2 mangoes (600g), cheeks sliced thinly

1 Place rice in a small bowl, cover with water; stand for 8 hours or overnight.

2 Drain rice; place in a small saucepan with pandan leaf, if using, and the water. Bring to the boil, reduce heat to medium; simmer for 20 minutes or until rice is tender and water is almost all absorbed.

3 Add half the coconut cream; cook for 10 minutes or until mixture thickens slightly. Add remaining coconut cream, syrup, coconut oil and salt; stir to combine well. Whisk in arrowroot; cook mixture for 3 minutes or until thickened.

4 Remove pandan leaf; discard. Transfer mixture to a large bowl, cover surface with plastic wrap; cool for 30 minutes or until at room temperature. Using a mortar and pestle crush sesame seeds (or see tip).

5 Transfer mixture to an ice-cream maker. Churn rice mixture in machine, following manufacturer's instructions, until thick; add three-quarters of the crushed sesame seeds, ½ teaspoon at a time, until just mixed through. Transfer mixture to a 1 litre (4-cup) capacity airtight container and freeze for at least 4 hours or until firm.

6 Serve scoops of ice-cream with mango, sprinkled with remaining sesame seeds.

TIP To crush sesame seeds without a mortar and pestle, place the seeds on a chopping board, press down on the seeds with a small heavy-based saucepan, using a twisting action.

TIP Use a good-
quality natural
peanut butter, made
from 100% peanuts.

RAW TWICKER BARS

PREP TIME **35 MINUTES (+ STANDING & FREEZING)** MAKES **20**

- 1 cup (140g) raw macadamias
- ½ cup (60g) pecans
- ¾ cup (60g) desiccated coconut
- ⅓ cup (70g) coconut oil, melted
- 1 tablespoon pure maple syrup
- ¼ teaspoon sea salt flakes

CARAMEL

- 9 fresh dates (180g), pitted
- ⅓ cup (95g) smooth natural peanut butter (see tips)
- ¼ cup (50g) coconut oil, melted
- ¼ cup (60ml) coconut cream
- ½ teaspoon sea salt flakes

CHOCOLATE COATING

- ¼ cup (50g) coconut oil
- ¼ cup (60g) cacao butter, chopped finely
- 2 tablespoons pure maple syrup
- ½ cup (50g) cacao powder

1 Make caramel.

2 Grease a 20cm (8-inch) square cake pan; line base and sides with baking paper, extending the paper 5cm (2 inches) over sides.

3 For raw shortbread layer, process nuts, desiccated coconut, oil, syrup and salt until mixture resembles coarse crumbs and starts to come together. Press firmly and evenly over base of pan using a spatula. Freeze for 20 minutes or until set.

4 Spread caramel over shortbread; smooth top with a spatula. Freeze for 1 hour or until set.

5 Remove carmel-topped shortbread from pan; cut into 20 bars, 10cm (4 inches) long and slightly less than 2cm (¾ inch) wide. Place on a baking-paper-lined tray; return to freezer until ready to coat.

6 Make chocolate coating.

7 Working one at a time, using tongs, dip bars in chocolate coating, turning to coat. Gently shake off excess chocolate; return to tray. Freeze for 10 minutes or until set.

8 Trim off any excess chocolate from bars. Using a spoon, drizzle remaining chocolate over bars. (If chocolate coating has thickened too much, reheat.) Freeze for 5 minutes or until chocolate is set.

CARAMEL

Place dates in a small bowl, cover with cold water. Stand for 30 minutes; drain. Blend drained dates with remaining ingredients until as smooth as possible, using a high-powered blender, if available; this type of blender will produce a very smooth consistency.

CHOCOLATE COATING

Place coconut oil and cacao butter in a medium heatproof bowl over a smaller heatproof bowl of boiling water, whisk until combined and smooth; whisk in syrup. Remove from heat; whisk in cacao until combined and smooth.

KEEPS Store bars in an airtight container in the fridge for up to 5 days or freeze for up to 2 months.

RAWTELLA PIE

PREP TIME 20 MINUTES (+ REFRIGERATION & FREEZING) SERVES 12

You will need to start this recipe a day ahead.

- 2 x 400ml cans coconut cream, unopened
- 2 cups (300g) raw cashews
- 1 cup (170g) activated buckwheat groats
- 1 cup (120g) pecans
- 5 fresh dates (100g), pitted
- ⅓ cup (35g) cacao powder
- 2 tablespoons pure maple syrup
- 2 tablespoons coconut oil, melted
- ½ cup (140g) chocolate hazelnut butter (see tips)
- ⅔ cup (160ml) coconut cream, extra
- ½ cup (125ml) pure maple syrup, extra
- ¼ cup (50g) coconut oil, melted, extra
- ¼ teaspoon natural hazelnut flavour (see tips)
- 1 teaspoon pure vanilla extract
- ¼ teaspoon sea salt flakes
- 60g (2 ounces) dark (semi-sweet) vegan chocolate, chopped coarsely
- ¼ cup (35g) roasted hazelnuts, chopped coarsely, optional (see swap out)

1 Chill coconut cream cans overnight in fridge, so that cream separates and sets on top.

2 Place cashews in a large bowl; cover with cold water. Stand, covered, for 4 hours or overnight. Drain cashews, rinse under cold water; drain well.

3 Grease a 22cm (9-inch) pie dish.

4 Process buckwheat, pecans, dates, ¼ cup of the cacao powder, syrup and coconut oil until mixture resembles coarse crumbs and starts to come together. Press mixture firmly and evenly over base of pan, using a spatula to smooth. Freeze while preparing filling.

5 Blend drained cashews with remaining cacao powder, chocolate hazelnut butter, extra coconut cream, extra syrup, extra oil, hazelnut flavour, vanilla and salt until as smooth as possible, using a high-powered blender if available; this type of blender will produce a very smooth consistency. Pour mixture over pie base; smooth top. Cover; freeze for 3 hours or until firm.

6 Without shaking or tipping the cans of coconut cream, carefully spoon out the thick coconut cream that has set on top. Beat cream in a small bowl with an electric mixer until soft peaks form; spoon on top of pie.

7 Place chocolate in a small heatproof bowl over a saucepan of gently simmering water (don't allow bowl to touch water), stir until just melted; drizzle chocolate over pie. Sprinkle pie with chopped hazelnuts, if you like.

SWAP OUT You can substitute 1½ cups (460g) coconut yoghurt for coconut cream. As the hazelnuts scattered over are roasted, they are not in fact raw — raw food purists can omit these or use activated hazelnuts instead.

KEEPS Store pie in an airtight container in the fridge for up to 5 days, or freeze without whipped cream, for up to 2 months.

TIPS Natural hazelnut flavour is available from selected health food stores or can be purchased online. We used Medicine Flower's natural hazelnut flavour. Use only 2 or 4 drops of hazelnut 'oil' or 'essence' or 1 teaspoon hazelnut 'extract'. Raw chocolate hazelnut butter is made from cocoa, hazelnuts and coconut nectar. It is available from health food stores.

ROASTED BERRY FROZEN YOGHURT LAYER LOAF

PREP + COOK TIME **45 MINUTES (+ FREEZING)** SERVES **8**

- 2 cups (300g) blueberries
- 2 cups (260g) strawberries
- 3 cups (840g) Greek-style yoghurt
- ⅔ cup (240g) rice malt syrup
- ½ cup (120g) mashed ripe banana
- ¼ cup (90g) honey
- ⅓ cup (40g) roasted almonds, chopped coarsely
- frozen or fresh cherries, strawberries and blueberries, to serve, optional

1 Preheat oven to 200°C/400°F. Line two large oven trays with baking paper. Line a 14cm x 24cm x 7cm (5½-inch x 9½-inch x 2¾-inch) loaf pan (1.5 litre/6 cups) with plastic wrap, extending the plastic 3cm (1¼ inches) over the side.
2 Place blueberries on one tray. Hull and quarter strawberries; place on other tray. Roast both berries for 18 minutes or until soft; cool on trays.
3 Process 1 cup (280g) of the yoghurt with ⅓ cup (120g) of the syrup. Pulse through blueberries until just combined. Pour into loaf tin; freeze for 45 minutes or until just frozen.
4 Meanwhile, stir banana and honey together in a medium bowl until smooth. Stir through 1 cup (280g) of remaining yoghurt and almonds. Pour over blueberry layer; freeze for 45 minutes or until just frozen.

5 Process strawberries and remaining syrup in cleaned blender. Add remaining yoghurt; pulse until just combined. Pour over banana layer; freeze for 3 hours or overnight.
6 Remove loaf from freezer 15 minutes before serving. Invert onto a chopping board, remove plastic wrap; cut into slices. Serve topped with cherries and extra berries.

SWAP OUT the almonds in the banana layer and replace with the same amount of toasted coconut flakes or coarsely chopped unsalted peanuts, if you like

COCONUT SUNDAE WITH CARAMEL POPCORN

PREP + COOK TIME **12 MINUTES** SERVES **4 (MAKES 6 CUPS CARAMEL POPCORN)**

- 1 tablespoon coconut oil
- ¼ cup (60g) popping corn
- ⅔ cup (160ml) coconut nectar
- ¼ cup (70g) cashew spread
- ½ teaspoon pure vanilla extract
- ½ teaspoon sea salt flakes
- 8 large scoops coconut and vanilla ice-cream (see page 46)
- 2 raw twicker bars (see page 189), broken in half, optional

CHOCOLATE SAUCE

- 1 tablespoon cacao powder
- 1½ tablespoons coconut oil, melted
- 1 tablespoon pure maple syrup

1 Preheat oven to 160°C/320°F. Line an oven tray with baking paper.

2 Heat coconut oil in a large saucepan over medium-high heat. Add popping corn, cover with a lid; shake pan lightly when kernels start to pop. Cook for 3 minutes or until kernels have popped, shaking pan regularly. Transfer to a large heatproof bowl; discard any uncooked kernels.

3 Combine coconut nectar, cashew spread, vanilla and salt in a medium bowl. Pour half the cashew caramel over popcorn; stir well to coat. Transfer the remaining cashew caramel to a jar or glass bottle with a lid until ready to serve sundaes.

4 Spoon popcorn mixture in an even layer onto oven tray; bake for 8 minutes or until golden brown, stirring occasionally to prevent popcorn from burning. Cool popcorn mixture on tray.

5 Make chocolate sauce.

6 Divide ice-cream among four ¾ cup (180ml) glasses; drizzle with remaining cashew caramel and chocolate sauce. Top evenly with caramel popcorn and raw twicker bars, if using.

CHOCOLATE SAUCE

Combine all ingredients in a small bowl.

KEEPS Store caramel popcorn in an airtight container in the pantry for up to 2 days. Store cashew caramel in a jar in the fridge for up to 1 week.

TIP If you don't
have time to make
your own ice-cream
or raw twicker bars,
simply make the
caramel popcorn and
chocolate sauce
and serve with your
favourite sugar-free
ice-cream.

TIP Freeze-dried
strawberry powder
is available from
some health food
stores and gourmet
food stores.

RAW STRAWBERRY CREAM COOKIES

PREP TIME 40 MINUTES (+ STANDING & FREEZING) MAKES 20

You will need to start this recipe a day ahead.

- 1 cup (140g) raw macadamias
- ¾ cup (90g) pecans
- ¾ cup (65g) desiccated coconut
- ⅓ cup (70g) coconut oil, melted
- 1 tablespoon raw honey
- ½ teaspoon pure vanilla extract

STRAWBERRY CREAM

- 1 cup (150g) raw cashews
- 250g (8 ounces) strawberries
- ½ cup (100g) coconut oil, melted
- ¼ cup (90g) raw honey
- 1 tablespoon freeze-dried strawberry powder (see tip), optional

CHOCOLATE COATING

- ¼ cup (50g) coconut oil
- ¾ cup (180g) cacao butter, chopped finely
- ⅓ cup (80ml) pure maple syrup
- ½ teaspoon pure vanilla extract
- 1 cup (100g) cacao powder

1 Place cashews for strawberry cream in a small bowl; cover with cold water. Stand, covered, for 4 hours or overnight. Drain cashews; rinse under cold water, drain well.

2 Make strawberry cream.

3 Grease a 20cm x 30cm (8-inch x 12-inch) slice pan; line with plastic wrap, extending plastic 5cm (2 inches) over sides.

4 Process macadamias, pecans, desiccated coconut, coconut oil, honey and vanilla until mixture resembles coarse crumbs and holds together when pressed; be careful not to over-process. Press nut mixture firmly and evenly over base of pan using a spatula. Freeze for 15 minutes or until firm.

5 Lift cookie base from pan; place on a chopping board. Cut base into 20 rounds using a 5cm (2-inch) cutter, pushing scraps together as necessary. Place rounds on baking paper-lined tray.

6 Spoon strawberry cream into piping bag fitted with a 1cm (½-inch) plain tube; pipe 5cm (2-inch) rounds on top of cookies, creating small peaks. Return cookies to freezer while you prepare chocolate coating.

7 Make chocolate coating.

8 Using a fork, lower cookies, one at a time, into chocolate coating. Spoon chocolate over; allow excess chocolate to drain off. Place cookies on tray; freeze for 10 minutes or until chocolate is set. Repeat process to coat cookies twice in chocolate coating, if necessary. If chocolate has thickened too much, reheat briefly. Return cookies to freezer for 10 minutes or until set. Trim off any excess chocolate.

STRAWBERRY CREAM

Blend drained cashews with remaining ingredients until as smooth as possible, using a high-powered blender, if available; this type of blender will achieve a very smooth consistency. Pour into a medium bowl; freeze for 1¼ hours or until very thick. Whisk vigorously until smooth.

CHOCOLATE COATING

Place coconut oil and cacao butter in a large heatproof bowl over a medium heatproof bowl of boiling water; whisk until combined and smooth. Whisk in syrup and vanilla; remove from heat. Whisk in cacao until combined and smooth.

KEEPS Store cookies in an airtight container in the fridge for up to 5 days or freeze for up to 2 months.

VIETNAMESE-STYLE COCONUT AFFOGATO

PREP TIME 25 MINUTES (+ STANDING & FREEZING) SERVES 2

- ¼ cup (15g) fresh ground coffee
- ¾ cup (180ml) boiling water
- toasted shaved coconut flakes, to serve, optional

CHEAT'S COCONUT ICE-CREAM

- 2 tablespoons desiccated coconut
- 1 vanilla bean
- 400ml can coconut cream
- ½ cup (125ml) pure maple syrup
- 1 tablespoon coconut oil, at room temperature
- ½ teaspoon sea salt flakes

1 Make cheat's coconut ice-cream.

2 Place coffee in a plunger, pour over the boiling water. Stand for 4 minutes; press down on grounds. Pour into two espresso cups. (Alternatively, combine the boiling water and coffee in a heatproof jug, stand for 4 minutes; strain through a fine sieve.)

3 Meanwhile, remove ice-cream from freezer. Allow to soften slightly. Process in a small blender until a soft-serve consistency. (For a smoother result, process frozen coconut mixture until smooth, return to the zip-top bag; re-freeze until frozen.)

4 To serve, spoon coconut ice-cream evenly into two 1½ cup (375ml) glasses. Sprinkle with shaved coconut. Accompany with the coffee for each person to pour over ice-cream before eating.

CHEAT'S COCONUT ICE-CREAM

Place desiccated coconut in a small frying pan over high heat. Stir with a wooden spoon for 1 minute or until golden and toasted. Transfer to a plate; leave to cool completely. Split vanilla bean lengthways; scrape seeds from halves, using the tip of a knife. Process vanilla seeds, coconut cream, syrup, coconut oil and salt until smooth. Remove blade, stir in toasted coconut; transfer to a large zip-top bag. Close bag, place on a metal tray, spread coconut mixture flat; freeze for 3 hours.

TIP Matcha is a type of green tea that has been blended into a fine powder. You can find it at specialty tea stores or Asian supermarkets.

MATCHA CHOC POPS

PREP + COOK TIME **15 MINUTES (+ FREEZING)** MAKES **10**

*You will need 10 x ½-cup (125ml) popsicle moulds and
10 paddle pop sticks for this recipe. The higher the
percentage of cocoa solids a chocolate contains,
the less room there is for additives, such as sugar,
and the more intense the chocolate flavour.*

- 1 litre (4 cups) coconut milk
- ⅔ cup (240g) honey
- 1 tablespoon matcha (green tea) powder
  (see tip)
- 80g (2½ ounces) raw, organic dark
  chocolate (85% cocoa)

1 Whisk coconut milk, honey and matcha in a large jug until combined. Pour among
10 x ½ cup (125ml) popsicle moulds. Freeze for 2 hours or until starting to firm.
Insert sticks two-thirds into the centre of each pop; freeze for 4 hours or
overnight until firm.
2 Place moulds in a bowl of room temperature water; pull sticks quickly to remove
pops from moulds. Transfer pops to a baking-paper-lined tray; return to freezer.
3 Place chocolate in a small heatproof bowl. Place bowl over a small saucepan
of simmering water (don't let water touch base of bowl); stir until smooth and
melted. Cool for 5 minutes. Working quickly, dip a spoon in chocolate; drizzle
widthways across pops. Freeze for 5 minutes or until chocolate is set.

PURPLE CRUSH PIE

PREP TIME **20 MINUTES (+ STANDING & FREEZING)** SERVES **12**

You will need to start this recipe a day ahead.

- 2 cups (300g) raw cashews
- 150g (4½ ounces) frozen raspberries
- 150g (4½ ounces) frozen blueberries
- ½ cup (125ml) rice malt syrup
- ¼ cup (60ml) coconut cream
- 1 tablespoon finely grated lemon rind
- ¼ cup (60ml) lemon juice
- ⅔ cup (140g) coconut oil, melted
- 1 cup (150g) fresh or frozen mixed berries, to serve

ALMOND BASE

- ½ cup (80g) natural almonds
- ½ cup (85g) activated buckwheat groats
- ⅓ cup (40g) almond meal
- ¼ cup (25g) cacao powder
- 2 tablespoons yacon syrup or rice malt syrup (see tips)
- 1 tablespoon coconut oil, melted
- 1 teaspoon pure vanilla extract

1 Place cashews in a medium bowl; cover with cold water. Stand, covered, for 4 hours or overnight. Drain cashews, rinse under cold water; drain well.
2 Meanwhile, thaw raspberries and blueberries in a medium bowl at room temperature for 1 hour; do not drain.
3 Grease a 20cm (8-inch) round sandwich or shallow cake pan.
4 Make almond base.
5 Blend drained cashews, thawed berries, syrup, coconut cream, rind and juice until well combined. Add coconut oil and blend until as smooth as possible, using a high-powered blender, if available; this type of blender will produce a very smooth consistency.
6 Pour two-thirds of filling mixture over base, smooth top; freeze for 4 hours or until set. Meanwhile, transfer remaining filling to a small bowl; refrigerate to firm while base sets.
7 Using a palette knife, spread remaining filling over pie, creating soft swirls.
8 Top with mixed berries just before serving.

ALMOND BASE
Process all ingredients until mixture resembles coarse crumbs and starts to come together. Press mixture firmly and evenly over base of pan, using a spatula. Freeze while preparing filling.

KEEPS Store pie in an airtight container in the fridge for up to 5 days or freeze the undecorated pie for up to 2 months.

TIP Yacon syrup is
available from some
health food stores.
It has a consistency
similar to rice malt
syrup, with a distinct
treacle-like flavour
and a mild level of
sweetness. It is
considered by many
to be one of the
healthiest sweeteners
available.

GINGER & SPICE
CRUMBLE TOPPING

*Orange & poppy
seed topping*

Cacao nib & coconut topping

SEEDS OF LIFE
TOPPING

BERRY CRUMBLE WITH TOPPING VARIATIONS
PREP + COOK TIME **40 MINUTES** SERVES **6**

Preheat oven to 180°C/350°F. Grease six 10cm (4-inch) diameter, 1¼ cup ovenproof dishes. Combine 4 cups fresh pitted cherries, 500g (1lb) fresh or frozen raspberries, scraped seeds from 1 vanilla bean, 2 tablespoons orange juice and 1 tablespoon pure maple syrup in a large bowl. Using your hands, squeeze ingredients together between your fingers until just combined; divide among dishes. Make your choice of topping below; sprinkle over fruit. Bake for 20 minutes or until topping is golden and fruit bubbling. Serve with cream, sugar-free yoghurt or ice-cream.

TIPS Freeze raw toppings for up to 3 months. Use straight from the freezer and bake for 25 minutes.

GINGER & SPICE CRUMBLE TOPPING
PREP + COOK TIME **10 MINUTES** MAKES **2 CUPS**

Place 1 cup almond meal, ½ cup rolled oats, 3 teaspoons ground ginger, 1 teaspoon mixed spice, ⅓ cup flaked almonds, 2 tablespoons pure maple syrup and 100g (3oz) finely chopped cold butter in a medium bowl. Using fingertips, rub mixture together until it resembles coarse breadcrumbs.

CACAO NIB & COCONUT TOPPING
PREP + COOK TIME **10 MINUTES** MAKES **2½ CUPS**

Place 1 cup hazelnut meal, ½ cup rolled oats, ¼ cup cacao nibs, ½ cup coconut flakes, 2 tablespoons pure maple syrup and 100g (3oz) firm coconut oil in a medium bowl. Using fingertips, rub mixture together until it resembles coarse breadcrumbs.

ORANGE & POPPY SEED TOPPING
PREP + COOK TIME **10 MINUTES** MAKES **2½ CUPS**

Place 1 cup almond meal, ½ cup rolled oats, 2 tablespoons coarsely chopped natural almonds, 2 tablespoons poppy seeds, 2 teaspoons finely grated orange rind, 100g (3oz) finely chopped cold butter and 2 tablespoons pure maple syrup in a medium bowl. Using fingertips, rub mixture together until it resembles coarse breadcrumbs.

SEEDS OF LIFE TOPPING
PREP + COOK TIME **10 MINUTES** MAKES **2¾ CUPS**

Place 1 cup almond meal, ½ cup quinoa flakes, ¼ cup pepitas, 2 tablespoons each chia and sesame seeds, 2 tablespoons pure maple syrup and 100g (3oz) finely chopped cold butter in a medium bowl. Using fingertips, rub mixture together until it resembles coarse breadcrumbs.

TIPS Dehydrated orange slices are available from some health food stores or, to make your own, see raw jaffa cake, page 211.

RAW CITRUS CHEESECAKE SLICE

PREP TIME **25 MINUTES (+ STANDING & FREEZING)** MAKES **14 SLICES**

You will need to start this recipe a day ahead.

- 3 cups (450g) raw cashews
- 1 cup (140g) raw macadamias
- ¾ cup (120g) natural almonds
- ½ cup (40g) desiccated coconut
- 6 fresh dates (120g), pitted
- ¼ teaspoon sea salt flakes
- ⅔ cup (160ml) rice malt syrup
- ⅓ cup (80ml) coconut cream
- ½ teaspoon pure vanilla extract
- 2 tablespoons finely grated lemon rind
- ⅓ cup (80ml) lemon juice
- 1 cup (200g) coconut oil, melted
- ½ teaspoon ground turmeric
- 2 tablespoons finely grated orange rind
- 2 tablespoons orange juice
- 2 tablespoons raw macadamias, extra, chopped finely
- 7 dehydrated orange slices, cut into quarters, optional (see tips)

1 Place cashews in a large bowl; cover with cold water. Stand, covered, for 4 hours or overnight. Drain cashews; rinse under cold water, drain well.

2 Grease an 18cm x 28cm (7¼-inch x 11¼-inch) slice pan; line base and sides with baking paper, extending paper 5cm (2 inches) over sides.

3 Process macadamias, almonds, desiccated coconut, dates and salt until mixture resembles coarse crumbs and starts to stick together; be careful not to over-process. Press nut mixture firmly and evenly over base of pan, using a spatula. Freeze until required.

4 To make lemon filling, blend drained cashews, syrup, coconut cream, vanilla, lemon rind and juice until well combined. Add ¾ cup of the coconut oil; blend until as smooth as possible, using a high-powered blender, if available; this type of blender will produce a very smooth consistency. Pour two-thirds of the lemon filling over base; smooth top. Freeze slice for 1 hour to firm slightly.

5 Add turmeric, orange rind and juice to the remaining lemon filling and blend until combined. Add remaining oil; blend until well combined. Pour orange filling over lemon layer; tilt pan to spread evenly. Freeze slice for 4 hours or until set.

6 Cut slice into 14 rectangles. Serve slice topped with extra chopped macadamias and dehydrated orange pieces, if you like.

KEEPS Store slice in an airtight container in the fridge for up to 5 days, or freeze for up to 2 months.

MILKY TEA COOKIE SANDWICH

PREP + COOK TIME **45 MINUTES (+ STANDING & COOLING)** MAKES **20**

- 2¼ cups (200g) traditional rolled oats
- ½ cup (40g) desiccated coconut
- ⅓ cup (40g) coarsely chopped pecans
- 1½ teaspoons ground ginger
- ½ cup (100g) coconut oil, melted
- ¼ cup (90g) honey
- ½ teaspoon sea salt flakes

MILKY TEA CREAM

- 4 english breakfast tea bags
- 1 cup (150g) raw cashews
- 2 cups (500ml) boiling water
- 1 tablespoon honey

1 Preheat oven to 180°C/350°F. Grease two large oven trays; line with baking paper.

2 Make milky tea cream.

3 Process oats, coconut, pecans, ginger, coconut oil, honey and salt for 2 minutes or until very finely chopped and thoroughly combined. Roll mixture out between two sheets of baking paper until 5mm (¼-inch) thick. (The mixture will look a little bit dry but will hold together during cooking.) Using a 5cm (2-inch) round cutter, cut out 40 rounds, re-rolling as necessary. Using a palette knife, transfer cookies to trays 1cm (½ inch) apart.

4 Bake for 8 minutes or until golden and a cookie can be pushed gently without breaking. Stand on trays for 10 minutes; transfer to a wire rack to cool.

5 Pipe approximately 2 teaspoons of milky tea cream onto half of the cookies; sandwich with remaining cookies.

MILKY TEA CREAM

Place 3 of the tea bags and cashews in a medium bowl. Cover with the boiling water; stand for 20 minutes. Strain over a bowl; reserve ⅓ cup (80ml) of the tea liquid. Discard soaked tea bags. Open remaining tea bag, measure ½ teaspoon tea leaves; discard remainder. In a small food processor, blend measured tea, soaked cashews, ¼ cup reserved tea liquid and honey until a smooth icing consistency; if too thick, blend with remaining 1 tablespoon reserved liquid. Spoon mixture into a piping bag fitted with a 1cm (½-inch) straight nozzle. Refrigerate 1 hour.

KEEPS Store filled cookies in an airtight container at room temperature for up to 3 days.

TIPS Activated buckwheat groats are available from health food stores; they add a delicious crunch. You can also buy dehydrated orange slices from some health food stores, if you prefer.

RAW CHOCOLATE JAFFA CAKE

PREP TIME **30 MINUTES (+ STANDING, REFRIGERATION, FREEZING & DEHYDRATION)** SERVES **16**

You will need to start this recipe a day ahead.

- ¾ cup (120g) natural almonds
- ⅓ cup (40g) almond meal
- ¼ cup (25g) cacao powder
- ½ cup (100g) activated buckwheat groats (see tips)
- ¼ cup (60ml) coconut nectar
- 20g (¾ ounce) coconut oil, melted
- ¾ teaspoon pure vanilla extract

CHOC-DIPPED ORANGE SLICES

- 1 medium orange (240g)
- 100g (3 ounces) vegan dark chocolate (70% cocoa), grated coarsely

FILLING

- 2 cups (300g) raw cashews
- ½ cup (125ml) pure maple syrup
- ½ cup (100g) coconut oil, melted
- ⅓ cup (35g) cacao powder
- 1½ tablespoons finely grated orange rind
- ¾ cup (180ml) fresh orange juice
- 40g (1½ ounces) cacao butter, melted
- ½ teaspoon pure vanilla extract

CHOCOLATE GANACHE

- ½ cup (50g) cacao powder
- ½ cup (125ml) pure maple syrup
- ¼ cup (50g) coconut oil, melted
- 1 teaspoon pure vanilla extract

1 Make choc-dipped orange slices and filling.
2 Grease a 23cm (9¼-inch) springform cake pan. Line base and side with baking paper.
3 Process both almonds and cacao until mixture resembles coarse crumbs. Add buckwheat groats, coconut nectar, oil and vanilla; process until just combined. Press nut mixture firmly and evenly over base of pan, using a spatula. Freeze for 15 minutes.
4 Pour filling over base; freeze for 2½ hours or until firm.
5 Make chocolate ganache. Pour over cake; smooth top. Refrigerate for 15 minutes or until set.
6 Remove cake from pan; place on a plate. Top with choc-dipped orange slices; serve.

CHOC-DIPPED ORANGE SLICES
Preheat dehydrator to 46°C/115°F. Cut orange into 3mm (⅛-inch) thick slices; remove any seeds. Arrange slices on mesh dehydrator trays. Dehydrate for 12-24 hours, turning slices halfway, or until slices are dry and brittle; the time will depend on the quality of dehydrator and juiciness of the orange. (Alternatively, preheat oven to its lowest temperature, ideally 50°C/122°F. Line an oven tray with baking paper; place a rectangular greased wire rack on top. Arrange orange slices on rack. Place tray in oven; leave

door slightly ajar so air can circulate and moisture can escape. Bake for 12 hours or until dry and brittle, turning slices occasionally.) Melt chocolate in a small heatproof bowl over a bowl of hot water. Dip orange slices halfway into chocolate; gently shake away excess chocolate. Place slices on a tray lined with baking paper; refrigerate for 15 minutes or until set. Leave some slices uncoated, if you prefer.

FILLING
Place cashews in a medium bowl; cover with cold water. Stand, covered, for 4 hours or overnight. Drain cashews, rinse under cold water; drain well. Blend cashews with remaining ingredients until as smooth as possible, using a high-powered blender, if available; this type of blender will produce a very smooth consistency.

CHOCOLATE GANACHE
Blend all the ingredients until smooth and silky.

KEEPS Store cake in an airtight container in the fridge for up to 5 days or freeze the undecorated cake for up to 2 months.

ORANGE-POMEGRANATE AND CHOCOLATE GRANITAS

PREP TIME 25 MINUTES (+ COOLING & FREEZING) SERVES 6

- 2 large pomegranates (860g)
- 2 cups (450ml) fresh strained orange juice
- 1 cup (360g) rice malt syrup
- 1 vanilla bean
- 3 cups (750ml) water
- 1 cup (100g) cacao powder
- ½ cup (125ml) pouring cream

1 For orange-pomegranate granita, cut or tear pomegranates in half crossways; scoop seeds out and place in a food processor bowl. Pulse for 10 seconds or until juice from seeds is released. Strain juice through a fine sieve over a medium bowl; you will need ⅔ cup (160ml) juice for the recipe.

2 Pour measured pomegranate juice, orange juice and ½ cup (180g) of the syrup into a medium saucepan. Bring to the boil over high heat, stirring until syrup dissolves. Pour mixture into a 4cm (1½-inch) deep, 22cm (9-inch) square cake pan. Cool for 15 minutes; freeze for 4 hours or until frozen.

3 For chocolate granita, split vanilla bean lengthways, scrape seeds from halves, using the tip of a knife. Add to a medium saucepan along with the water, cacao and the remaining syrup. Bring to the boil, reduce heat to low; simmer, whisking, for 2 minutes or until cacao is dissolved. Stir in cream. Pour into a 4cm (1½-inch) deep, 22cm (9-inch) square cake pan. Cool for 15 minutes; freeze for 4 hours or until frozen.

4 Remove both granitas from freezer. Using a fork, break up the ice crystals; return to freezer until ready to serve.

5 Remove granitas from freezer 10 minutes before serving. Layer granitas in small glasses or bowls; top with extra pomegranate seeds, if you like.

TIP Try replacing
pomegranate juice
with ¾ cup (180ml)
freshly squeezed
blood orange juice,
when in season;
strain the juice
to remove any pulp,
which may affect
the granita texture.

SPICED PEAR CHEESECAKE

PREP + COOK TIME **1 HOUR 15 MINUTES (+ STANDING & FREEZING)** SERVES **16**

You will need to start this recipe a day ahead.

- 2 cups (300g) raw cashews
- 1 cup (140g) raw macadamias
- 5 medium brown pears (1.2kg), such as beurre bosc
- ½ cup (125ml) coconut nectar
- 1½ cups (180g) pecans
- ½ cup (50g) walnuts
- ½ cup dried figs (100g), chopped finely
- ⅛ teaspoon sea salt flakes
- 130g (4½ ounce) piece fresh ginger, grated finely
- 1 cup (250ml) coconut cream
- ⅓ cup (80ml) coconut nectar, extra
- 2 teaspoons pure vanilla extract
- 2½ teaspoons ground cinnamon
- ¾ cup (150g) coconut oil, melted
- 1 tablespoon freeze-dried rose petals, optional
- 2 teaspoons cacao nibs, optional

1 Place cashews and macadamias in a large bowl; cover with cold water. Stand, covered, for 4 hours or overnight. Drain nuts; rinse under cold water; drain well.

2 Preheat oven to 160°C/320°F. Grease a 22cm (9-inch) springform cake pan. Line three oven trays with baking paper.

3 Peel and cut three of the pears into 1cm (½-inch) cubes; place on one oven tray. Drizzle with ⅓ cup of the nectar; toss to coat evenly. Bake for 40 minutes or until tender. Transfer to a wire rack to cool.

4 Thinly slice remaining pears lengthways with a mandoline or sharp knife. Place slices in a single layer on remaining oven trays. Drizzle with remaining nectar; turn to evenly coat. Bake for 20 minutes. Turn slices; bake for a further 15 minutes or until dark golden brown; (check frequently to ensure they do not burn). Transfer to a wire rack to cool completely. Store in an airtight container until ready to serve.

5 Process pecans, walnuts, fig and salt until fine crumbs form. Press mixture over base of cake pan; use the back of a spoon to press down firmly and smooth surface. Freeze while preparing filling.

6 Press grated ginger through a fine sieve over a small bowl; you will need ¼ cup (60ml) ginger juice. Discard pulp. Blend ginger juice with drained cashews and macadamias, coconut cream, extra nectar, vanilla and 2 teaspoons of the cinnamon until well combined. Add coconut oil; blend until as smooth as possible, using a high-powered blender, if available; this type of blender will produce a very smooth consistency.

7 Pour half the filling mixture over base. Scatter with diced pear; press a few of the pear pieces lightly into filling. Pour remaining filling over to cover pear; smooth top. Freeze cake for 5 hours or until set.

8 Sift remaining cinnamon over top of cake, arrange pear slices on top; scatter with rose petals and cacao nibs.

SWAP OUT You can use 2 cups pecans instead of 1½ cups pecans and ½ cup walnuts.

KEEPS Store cake in an airtight container in the fridge for up to 5 days or freeze the undecorated cake for up to 2 months. Store baked pear slices in a container in the pantry for up to 1 week.

RAW GINGERBREAD APPLE CUPCAKES

PREP + COOK TIME 15 MINUTES (+ REFRIGERATION) MAKES 12

You will need to start the labneh recipe a day ahead. These cupcakes are gluten-free; to make them dairy-free, follow the tips in 'swap out'.

- 1½ cups (130g) dried apple slices
- 3 cups (330g) coarsely chopped walnuts
- 12 fresh dates (240g), pitted
- 60g (2 ounces) butter, melted
- 1 tablespoon finely grated fresh ginger
- 1½ teaspoons pure vanilla extract
- ½ teaspoon sea salt flakes
- ½ teaspoon mixed spice
- 2 tablespoons coarsely chopped dried apple slices, extra
- 2 tablespoons freeze-dried rose petals, optional

SPICED HONEY LABNEH

- 2 cups (560g) Greek-style yoghurt
- 1½ tablespoons raw honey
- 1½ teaspoons finely grated fresh ginger

1 Make spiced honey labneh.

2 Line a 12-hole (⅓ cup/80ml) muffin tin with paper cases.

3 Place apple slices in a medium bowl; cover with boiling water. Stand for 5 minutes; drain, reserving 1½ tablespoons of the soaking water.

4 Process apple, reserved water, walnuts, dates, butter, ginger, vanilla, salt and ¼ teaspoon of the mixed spice until well combined. Press evenly into paper cases; cover with plastic wrap and refrigerate for at least 4 hours or overnight until firm.

5 Top cupcakes with spiced honey labneh. Sprinkle with remaining mixed spice, extra chopped dried apple and rose petals, if you like.

SPICED HONEY LABNEH

Line a small sieve with muslin (or a clean loosely-woven cotton cloth); place sieve over a medium bowl. Spoon yoghurt into lined sieve; cover and refrigerate overnight. Transfer labneh to a bowl. Stir in honey and ginger. Cover with plastic wrap; refrigerate until required.

SWAP OUT apple and replace with dried pears. To make a dairy-free version, substitute coconut oil for butter and unsweetened coconut yoghurt for the spiced honey labneh.

KEEPS Store cupcakes in an airtight container in the fridge for up to 1 week.

TIPS Try this with peanuts sprinkled over the top before serving or drizzled with salted caramel sauce (see page 81) or melted vegan salted caramel chocolate.

RAW CHOC-PEANUT CAKE

PREP TIME 55 MINUTES (+ STANDING, FREEZING & REFRIGERATION) SERVES 16

You will need to start this recipe a day ahead.

- ½ cup (80g) natural almonds
- ¾ cup (90g) almond meal
- ¾ cup (60g) desiccated coconut
- ¼ cup (60ml) pure maple syrup
- 2 tablespoons almond butter
- ⅓ cup (40g) cacao powder
- ¼ teaspoon pure vanilla extract
- 1 cup (140g) roasted unsalted peanuts, chopped coarsely

NOUGAT

- 2½ cups (375g) raw cashews
- 1 cup (250ml) coconut cream
- ½ cup (125ml) pure maple syrup
- ½ cup (130g) almond butter
- 1 cup (80g) desiccated coconut
- ½ cup (100g) coconut oil, melted
- ½ teaspoon pure vanilla extract

CARAMEL

- 1 cup (140g) fresh dates, pitted
- ½ cup (140g) smooth peanut butter
- ¼ cup (60ml) coconut cream
- ¼ cup (50g) coconut oil, melted
- 1 tablespoon pure maple syrup
- ¼ teaspoon fine sea salt

CHOCOLATE COATING

- ¼ cup (50g) coconut oil
- ¼ cup (60g) cacao butter, chopped finely
- ¼ cup (60ml) pure maple syrup
- ⅔ cup (70g) cacao powder

1 Make nougat.

2 Grease a 23cm (9¼-inch) springform cake pan. Line base and side with baking paper.

3 Process almonds until coarsely chopped. Add almond meal, coconut, syrup, almond butter, 2 tablespoons of the cacao powder and vanilla; process until combined and mixture starts to stick together. Press mixture over base of pan; smooth surface. Freeze until required.

4 Pour two-thirds of the nougat over base; freeze for 30 minutes.

5 Add remaining cacao powder to the remaining nougat mixture; blend until well combined. Spread over nougat layer; smooth top. Freeze for 3 hours or until firm.

6 Make caramel. Spread caramel over cake; sprinkle with chopped peanuts. Freeze for 30 minutes or until caramel firms up slightly.

7 Make chocolate coating.

8 Remove cake from pan; place on a plate. Drizzle chocolate coating over cake, allowing it to drip down the sides. Using a palette knife, smooth coating over cake. Refrigerate for 30 minutes or until set.

NOUGAT

Place cashews in a medium bowl; cover with cold water. Stand, covered, for 4 hours or overnight. Drain cashews, rinse under cold water; drain well. Blend drained cashews with coconut cream, syrup and almond butter until as smooth as possible, using a high-powered blender, if available; this type of blender will produce a very smooth consistency. Add remaining ingredients; blend until well combined.

CARAMEL

Place dates in a small bowl; add enough cold water to cover. Stand for 30 minutes, drain. Blend soaked dates with remaining ingredients until as smooth as possible, using a high-powered blender, if available; this type of blender will produce a very smooth consistency.

CHOCOLATE COATING

Place coconut oil and cacao butter in a large heatproof bowl over a medium heatproof bowl of boiling water, whisk until combined and smooth; whisk in syrup. Whisk in cacao until combined and smooth.

KEEPS Store the cake in an airtight container in the fridge for up to 5 days or frozen for up to 2 months.

RAW BLUEBERRY LEMON CHEESECAKE

PREP TIME **30 MINUTES (+ STANDING & FREEZING)** SERVES **12**

You will need to start this recipe a day ahead.

- 3 cups (450g) raw cashews
- 1 cup (140g) macadamias
- ½ cup (40g) desiccated coconut
- 5 fresh dates (100g), pitted
- ½ cup (60g) pecans
- ¼ teaspoon fine sea salt
- ⅓ cup (80ml) coconut cream
- ⅔ cup (160ml) pure maple syrup or ½ cup (125ml) light agave syrup
- 1½ tablespoons finely grated lemon rind
- ⅓ cup (80ml) lemon juice
- ½ teaspoon pure vanilla extract
- ⅔ cup (140g) coconut oil, melted
- 40g (1½ ounces) cacao butter, melted
- 1½ cups (225g) frozen blueberries
- 125g (4 ounces) fresh blueberries
- 1 large lemon, sliced thinly crossways

1 Place cashews in a medium bowl; cover with cold water. Stand, covered, for 4 hours or overnight. Drain cashews, rinse under cold water; drain well.

2 Grease a 20cm (8-inch) springform cake pan. Line base and side with baking paper.

3 Process macadamias, desiccated coconut and dates until mixture resembles coarse crumbs. Add pecans and salt; process until combined and mixture starts to stick together. Press nut mixture firmly and evenly over base of pan, using a spatula. Freeze until required.

4 Blend drained cashews, coconut cream, syrup, rind, juice and vanilla until as smooth as possible, using a high-powered blender, if available; this type of blender will produce a very smooth consistency. Add oil and cacao butter; process until well combined and completely smooth.

5 Pour two-thirds of the lemon filling over base; smooth top. Sprinkle with ½ cup frozen blueberries; press berries lightly into filling. Freeze for 1 hour to firm slightly.

6 Meanwhile, thaw remaining frozen blueberries. Add blueberries and any juice to remaining lemon filling; blend until as smooth as possible, using a clean and dry high-powered blender, if available; this type of blender will produce a very smooth consistency. Spread blueberry filling over lemon filling; smooth top. Freeze cake for 4 hours or until firm.

7 Remove cake from pan; place on a plate. Serve topped with fresh blueberries, and lemon slices.

SWAP OUT the frozen and fresh blueberries in the recipe with the same quantities of mixed berries, if you like.

KEEPS Store cake in an airtight container in the fridge for up to 5 days. The undecorated cake can be frozen in a container for up to 2 months.

TIPS If available, use organic almonds. In summer, soak almonds in the fridge. Nut bags are available from some health food stores and gourmet grocers. Freeze the almond pulp for another use; it can be used in dips, cookies and cakes, and to thicken curries and stews.

CLASSIC VANILLA MYLK

PREP TIME **10 MINUTES (+ STANDING)** MAKES **3 CUPS (750ML)**

You will need to start this recipe a day ahead.

- 1 cup (160g) natural almonds
  (see tips)
- pinch fine sea salt
- 3 cups (750ml) filtered water
- 1 vanilla bean

1 Place almonds and salt in a large bowl; cover with cold water. Stand, covered, for 8 hours or overnight. Drain almonds; rinse under cold water, drain well.
2 Blend almonds with the filtered water until smooth. Pour mixture through a nut bag (or strainer lined with a fine cloth) into a large jug; squeeze nut bag to release all the mylk. Split vanilla bean lengthways, scrape seeds into mylk; stir to combine.

KEEPS Store almond mylk in a sealed glass bottle in the fridge for up to 3 days.

STRAWBERRY MYLK

Choc-peanut mylkshake

LATTE
SHAKE

STRAWBERRY MYLK

PREP TIME **15 MINUTES (+ STANDING)** SERVES **2 (MAKES 400ML)**

Make classic vanilla mylk on page 223. Blend 1 cup of the chilled mylk with 1 cup fresh or frozen strawberries, 1 tablespoon cashew spread and 1 tablespoon raw honey.

<u>TIP</u> Pair with strawberry cream cookies (see page 197).

CHOC-PEANUT MYLKSHAKE

PREP TIME **20 MINUTES (+ STANDING)** SERVES **2 (MAKES 400ML)**

Make classic vanilla mylk on page 223. Make chocolate sauce. Blend 1 cup of the chilled mylk with 2 scoops coconut and vanilla ice-cream (see page 46) or ⅓ cup unsweetened coconut yoghurt, 3 pitted fresh dates, 2 tablespoons natural peanut butter and 1 tablespoon cacao powder until smooth. Drizzle 1½ tablespoons chocolate sauce around the inside of two ¾ cup glasses or bottles, before pouring in mylkshake.

<u>CHOCOLATE SAUCE</u>

Combine 1 tablespoon cacao powder, 1 tablespoon melted coconut oil and 1 tablespoon pure maple syrup in a small bowl.

LATTE SHAKE

PREP TIME **15 MINUTES (+ STANDING)** SERVES **2 (MAKES 400ML)**

Make classic vanilla mylk on page 223. Blend 1 cup of the chilled mylk with ⅓ cup chilled espresso or strong coffee, 2 scoops coconut and vanilla ice-cream (see page 46) or ⅓ cup unsweetened coconut yoghurt and 1 pitted fresh date until smooth. Serve shake topped with an extra scoop of coconut and vanilla ice-cream or your favourite sugar-free ice-cream, if you like.

RAW COOKIES AND CREAM SLICE

PREP TIME **25 MINUTES (+ STANDING & FREEZING)** MAKES **16**

You will need to start this recipe a day ahead.

- ¾ cup (115g) raw cashews
- ¾ cup (130g) activated buckwheat groats
- ¾ cup (120g) natural almonds
- ⅔ cup (50g) desiccated coconut
- ½ cup (50g) cacao powder
- ⅓ cup (80ml) pure maple syrup
- ¾ cup (150g) coconut oil, melted
- ½ teaspoon pure vanilla extract
- 2 young drinking coconuts (2.4kg)
- 1 cup (250ml) coconut cream
- ⅓ cup (80ml) rice malt syrup
- 2 teaspoons pure vanilla extract, extra

1 Place cashews in a small bowl; cover with cold water. Stand, covered, for 4 hours or overnight. Drain cashews, rinse under cold water; drain well.

2 Grease a 20cm (8-inch) square cake pan; line base and sides with baking paper, extending the paper 5cm (2 inches) over sides. Line an oven tray with baking paper.

3 Process buckwheat, almonds, desiccated coconut, cacao powder, maple syrup, ¼ cup of the coconut oil and vanilla until mixture resembles coarse crumbs and just starts to come together; be careful not to over-process. Press two-thirds of mixture firmly into lined pan, using a spatula. Press remaining mixture into a 1cm (½ inch) thick rectangle on lined tray. Freeze while preparing cream filling.

4 Place a coconut on its side on a chopping board. Carefully cut off the dome-shaped top with a cleaver or large knife; you will need to use a bit of force. Drain coconut water into a large jug. Spoon out the soft flesh. Repeat with remaining coconut; you should have approximately 2 cups (180g) coconut flesh (reserve coconut water for another use, see tip).

5 Blend coconut flesh, drained cashews, coconut cream, rice malt syrup and extra vanilla until smooth, using a high-powered blender, if available; this type of blender will produce a very smooth consistency. Add remaining coconut oil; blend until as smooth as possible. Pour over biscuit base in square pan.

6 Place biscuit rectangle from tray onto a cutting board, cut into 1cm (½ inch) pieces. Sprinkle pieces over cream filling, pressing lightly into filling. Freeze for 5 hours or until set.

7 Remove slice from pan 10 minutes before serving to soften slightly. Cut into 16 squares.

KEEPS Store slice in an airtight container in the fridge for up to 5 days or freeze for up to 2 months.

TIP Use the reserved
coconut juice in your
next smoothie.

CITRUS, ORANGE BLOSSOM AND BEAN CAKE

PREP + COOK TIME **1 HOUR 10 MINUTES (+ COOLING & STANDING)** SERVES **8**

- 400g (12½ ounces) canned cannellini beans, drained, rinsed
- 3 teaspoons orange blossom water
- 2 teaspoons finely grated orange rind
- 2 teaspoons finely grated lemon rind
- 1 vanilla bean, split lengthways, seeds scraped
- ½ cup (125ml) olive oil
- 3 eggs, separated
- ⅓ cup (115g) raw honey

- 1½ cups (180g) almond meal
- 2 teaspoons baking powder
- strips of orange and lemon rind, to decorate (optional)

HONEY-WHIPPED CREAM

- ¾ cup (180ml) thickened cream
- 1 tablespoon raw honey
- ¼ cup (70g) Greek-style yoghurt

1 Preheat oven to 160°C/325°F. Grease a 20cm (8-inch) round cake pan; line base and side with baking paper.

2 Process beans, orange blossom water, grated citrus rind, vanilla seeds, oil and egg yolks until smooth. Transfer to a large bowl.

3 Beat egg whites in a medium bowl with an electric mixer until soft peaks form. With the motor operating, gradually add honey; beat until stiff peaks form. Fold egg white mixture, almond meal and baking powder into bean mixture until combined to form a batter. Spoon batter into pan; smooth top.

4 Bake cake for 55 minutes or until a skewer inserted into the centre comes out clean. Cool cake in pan.

5 Make honey-whipped cream.

6 Spread honey-whipped cream over cooled cake. Serve sprinkled with citrus rind strips, if you like.

HONEY-WHIPPED CREAM

Beat all ingredients in a small bowl with an electric mixer until soft peaks form.

TIPS Serve topped with edible flowers, such as nasturtiums, if you like.

SWAP OUT the oranges and replace with tangelos or mandarins. To make this dairy-free, replace the honey-whipped cream with whipped coconut cream.

KEEPS Store cake in an airtight container in the fridge for up to 2 days or freeze un-iced cake for up to 1 month.

PEPPERMINT BITES

PREP TIME **45 MINUTES (+ STANDING, FREEZING & REFRIGERATION)** MAKES **20**

You will need to start this recipe a day ahead.

- ¾ cup (115g) raw cashews
- ½ cup (80g) natural almonds
- ½ cup (60g) pecans
- ⅓ cup (65g) activated buckwheat groats (see tips)
- ⅔ cup (50g) desiccated coconut
- ½ cup (50g) cacao powder
- ¼ cup (40g) coconut sugar
- 4 fresh dates (80g), pitted
- ⅔ cup (140g) coconut oil, melted
- ¼ cup (60ml) coconut cream
- 2 tablespoons light agave syrup
- ½ teaspoon pure peppermint extract (see tips)

CHOCOLATE COATING

- ¼ cup (50g) coconut oil
- 60g (2 ounces) cacao butter, grated finely
- 2 tablespoons pure maple syrup
- ½ cup (50g) cacao powder

1 Place cashews in a medium bowl; cover with cold water. Stand, covered, for 4 hours or overnight. Drain cashews, rinse under cold water; drain well.

2 Lightly grease or oil a 20cm x 30cm (8-inch x 12-inch) slice pan; line with plastic wrap, extending plastic 5cm (2 inches) over sides.

3 Pulse almonds, pecans, groats, desiccated coconut, cacao, coconut sugar, dates and ½ cup of the oil until coarse crumbs form and mixture starts to come together; be careful not to over-process. Press nut mixture firmly and evenly over base of pan, using a spatula. Freeze for 15 minutes or until firm.

4 Lift biscuit base from pan; place on board. Cut base into 20 rounds using a 5cm (2-inch) cutter. Place rounds on a baking paper-lined tray; freeze while preparing peppermint cream.

5 To make peppermint cream, blend drained cashews with remaining coconut oil, coconut cream and syrup until as smooth as possible, using a high-powered blender, if available; this type of blender will produce a very smooth consistency. Add extract; blend until combined. Pour peppermint cream into a small bowl; cover, freeze for 1 hour or until thick but not set, stirring occasionally.

6 Spoon approximately 2 teaspoons of peppermint cream onto each biscuit round; using the back of the teaspoon, gently press down to flatten and smooth. Freeze for 3 hours or until set.

7 Make chocolate coating. Using a fork, lower biscuits, one at a time, into chocolate mixture. Allow excess chocolate to drain off, then place on tray. Refrigerate for 30 minutes or until chocolate is set.

CHOCOLATE COATING

Place coconut oil and cacao butter in a medium heatproof bowl over a smaller heatproof bowl of boiling water, whisk until combined and smooth; whisk in syrup. Whisk in cacao until combined and smooth.

KEEPS Store biscuits in an airtight container in the fridge for up to 5 days.

TIPS Activated buckwheat groats are available from health food stores; they add a delicious crunch. Peppermint extract is available from health food stores. Buy peppermint extract rather than oil or essence, otherwise the flavour of the biscuits may be affected.

TIPS Some dried
fruit, such as
Craisins and often
dried blueberries,
contain added sugar,
so avoid these if
you don't want to
use dried cherries.
Instead, use sultanas
and chopped dried figs
as a substitute.

✳ The unlikely secret ingredient in these gluten-free biscuits is black beans. It makes the cookies moist and fudge-like and means you are getting a really nutritious snack.

SECRET-INGREDIENT DARK CHOCOLATE CHERRY FUDGE COOKIES

PREP + COOK TIME **25 MINUTES** MAKES **12**

- 400g (1½ ounces) canned black beans, drained, rinsed
- 4 fresh pitted dates (80g)
- 2 tablespoons coconut oil, at room temperature
- ½ cup (50g) cacao powder
- 2 eggs
- ¼ cup (60ml) pure maple syrup
- 1 teaspoon pure vanilla extract
- ¼ cup (50g) dried cherries, chopped coarsely
- 100g (3½ ounces) sugar-free dark chocolate, chopped coarsely
- ¼ teaspoon sea salt flakes

1 Preheat oven to 200°C/400°F. Line two oven trays with baking paper.
2 Process beans, dates, coconut oil and cacao until smooth. Add eggs, maple syrup, vanilla and cherries; pulse until just combined. Stir through chocolate.
3 Spoon approximately 2 tablespoonfuls at a time onto trays, leaving 4cm (1½ inches) between cookies to allow for spreading. Sprinkle evenly with salt.
4 Bake for 12 minutes or until cookie edges are firm. Cool on trays.

KEEPS Store cookies in an airtight container for up to 2 days.

GLOSSARY

ACTIVATED BUCKINIS made with buckwheat, which, despite its name, is not actually a wheat, but is a fruit belonging to the same family as strawberries. It's gluten free, high in protein and essential amino acids, and is a rich source of minerals and B vitamins.

AGAVE SYRUP pronounced ah-GAH-vay. Also known as agave nectar; a sweetener produced from the agave plant in South Africa and Mexico (a succulent with thick fleshy leaves, each ending generally in a sharp point and having spiny edges; it is the plant from which tequila is made).

ALMONDS

meal also called ground almonds; almonds are powdered to a coarse flour-like texture.

flaked paper-thin slices.

slivered small pieces cut lengthways.

ARROWROOT a starch made from the rhizome of a Central American plant, used mostly as a thickening agent.

BAKING POWDER a raising agent consisting mainly of two parts cream of tartar to one part bicarbonate of soda.

BEANS

black also called turtle beans or black kidney beans; an earthy-flavoured dried bean completely different from the better-known Chinese black beans (fermented soybeans). Used mostly in Mexican and South American cooking.

borlotti also called roman beans or pink beans, can be eaten fresh or dried. Interchangeable with pinto beans due to their similarity in appearance - pale pink or beige with dark red streaks.

cannellini small white bean similar in appearance and flavour to other phaseolus vulgaris varieties (great northern, navy or haricot). Available dried or canned.

green also known as french or string beans (although the tough string they once had has generally been bred out of them), this long thin fresh bean is consumed in its entirety once cooked.

sprouts tender new growths of assorted beans and seeds germinated for consumption as sprouts.

BEETROOT (BEETS) also known as red beets; firm, round root vegetable.

BICARBONATE OF SODA (BAKING SODA) a raising agent.

BROCCOLINI a cross between broccoli and chinese kale; it has long stems with a long loose floret, both are completely edible. Resembles broccoli but is milder and sweeter in taste.

BUTTER use salted or unsalted (sweet) butter; 125g is equal to one stick of butter (4 ounces).

CACAO

beans are contained inside the large cacao pod. The beans are used to make cocoa butter, cocoa powder, cocoa solids and chocolate.

cacao (cocoa) butter is rich in saturated fats; about a third is stearic acid, but this acts differently to other saturated fats in that it doesn't raise cholesterol and, in fact, lowers LDL (bad) cholesterol. So this makes it a pretty healthy fat overall.

nibs can be separated into cocoa butter and powder. Cocoa powder retains many beneficial antioxidants and is an easy way of adding cocoa into your diet without the kilojoules of chocolate.

raw cacao powder is made by removing the cocoa butter using a process known as cold-pressing. It retains more of its nutrients than heat-processed cocoa powder; it also has a stronger, slightly bitter, taste.

raw dark chocolate is made using cold-pressed raw cacao beans, that is, without the use of heat. It is high in antioxidants, and has good levels of chromium, iron and magnesium, which support healthy heart function.

CHEESE

fetta Greek in origin; a crumbly textured goat- or sheep-milk cheese having a sharp, salty taste. Ripened and stored in salted whey; particularly good cubed and tossed into salads.

goat's made from goat's milk, has an earthy, strong taste; available in both soft and firm textures, in various shapes and sizes, and sometimes rolled in ash or herbs.

parmesan also called parmigiano; is a hard, grainy cow-milk cheese originating in Italy. Reggiano is the best variety.

ricotta a soft, sweet, moist, white cow-milk cheese with a low fat content and a slightly grainy texture. The name roughly translates as 'cooked again' and refers to ricotta's manufacture from a whey that is itself a by-product of other cheese making.

CHICKPEAS (GARBANZO BEANS) also called hummus or channa; an irregularly round, sandy-coloured legume. Firm texture even after cooking, a floury mouth-feel and robust nutty flavour; available canned or dried (reconstitute for several hours in cold water before use).

CHILLI available in many different types and sizes. Use rubber gloves when seeding and chopping fresh chillies as they can burn your skin. Removing seeds and membranes lessens the heat level.

cayenne pepper a long, thin-fleshed, extremely hot red chilli usually sold dried and ground.

chipotle pronounced cheh-pote-lay. The name used for jalapeño chillies once they've been dried and smoked. Having a deep, intensely smokey flavour, rather than a searing heat, chipotles are dark brown, almost black in colour and wrinkled in appearance.

flakes also sold as crushed chilli; dehydrated deep-red extremely fine slices and whole seeds.

green any unripened chilli; also some particular varieties that are ripe when green, such as jalapeño, habanero, poblano or serrano.

jalapeño pronounced hah-lah-pain-yo. Fairly hot, medium-sized, plump, dark green chilli; available pickled, sold canned or bottled, and fresh, from greengrocers.

long available both fresh and dried; a generic term used for any moderately hot, thin, long (6-8cm/2¼-3¼ inch) chilli.

red thai also known as 'scuds'; small, very hot and bright red; can be substituted with fresh serrano or habanero chillies.

CINNAMON available in sticks (quills) and ground into powder; used as a sweet, fragrant flavouring in sweet and savoury foods.

COCONUT

cream comes from the first pressing of the coconut flesh, without the addition of water; the second pressing (less rich) is sold as coconut milk. Look for coconut cream labelled as 100% coconut, without added emulsifiers.

flaked dried flaked coconut flesh.

milk not the liquid found inside the fruit (coconut water), but the diluted liquid from the second pressing of the white flesh of a mature coconut (the first pressing produces coconut cream).

oil is extracted from the coconut flesh so you don't get any of the fibre, protein or carbohydrates present in the whole coconut. The best quality is virgin coconut oil, which is the oil pressed from the dried coconut flesh, and doesn't include the use of solvents or other refining processes.

shredded thin strips of dried coconut.

sugar is not made from coconuts, but from the sap of the blossoms of the coconut palm tree. It also has the same amount of kilojoules as regular table (white) sugar.

young are coconuts that are not fully mature. As a coconut ages, the amount of juice inside decreases, until it eventually disappears and is replaced by air.

CORIANDER (CILANTRO) a bright-green leafy herb with a pungent flavour. Both the stems and roots of coriander are also used in cooking; wash well before using. Also available ground or as seeds; these should not be substituted for fresh coriander as the tastes are completely different.

CORNFLOUR (CORNSTARCH) available made from corn or wheat (wheaten cornflour, which contains gluten, gives a lighter texture in cakes); used as a thickening agent in cooking.

CREAM, POURING also called pure or fresh cream. It has no additives and contains a minimum fat content of 35%.

DATES fruit of the date palm tree, eaten fresh or dried, on their own or in dishes. About 4-6cm (1½-2¼ inches) in length, oval and plump, thin-skinned, with a sweet flavour and sticky texture.

EGGPLANT also known as aubergine. Ranging in size from tiny to very large and in colour from pale green to deep purple.

FENNEL also known as finocchio or anise; a white to very pale green-white vegetable about 8-12cm in diameter. Also the name given to dried seeds having a licorice flavour.

FLOUR

buckwheat not actually a form of wheat, but a herb in the same plant family as rhubarb; it is gluten-free. Has a strong nutty taste.

chickpea (besan) made from ground chickpeas so is gluten-free and high in protein. Used in Indian cooking.

coconut see *Coconut*

plain (all-purpose) an all-purpose wheat flour.

self-raising plain flour sifted with baking powder in the proportion of 1 cup flour to 2 teaspoons baking powder.

rice very fine, almost powdery, gluten-free flour; made from ground white rice.

GINGER

fresh also called green or root ginger; the thick gnarled root of a tropical plant.

ground also called powdered ginger; used as a flavouring in baking but cannot be substituted for fresh ginger.

pickled pink or red coloured paper-thin shavings of ginger in a mixture of vinegar, sugar and natural colouring; used in Japanese cooking.

HAZELNUTS also known as filberts; plump, grape-sized, rich, sweet nut having a brown skin that is removed by rubbing heated nuts together vigorously in a tea-towel.

meal is made by grounding the hazelnuts to a coarse flour texture for use in baking or as a thickening agent.

LINSEEDS also known as flaxseeds, they are the richest plant source of omega 3 fats, which are essential for a healthy brain, heart, joints and immune system.

MAPLE SYRUP, PURE distilled from the sap of sugar maple trees found only in Canada and the USA. Maple-flavoured syrup or pancake syrup is not an adequate substitute for the real thing.

MATCHA finely ground green tea powder. Matcha is rich in antioxidants called polyphenols, which have been linked to prevention against heart disease and cancer. Made from the whole ground tea leaf, matcha contains three times the amount of caffeine than in a cup of steeped tea, instead being comparable to that of a cup of coffee.

MISO fermented soybean paste. There are many types of miso, each with its own aroma, flavour, colour and texture; it can be kept, airtight, for up to a year in the fridge.

NORI a type of dried seaweed used in Japanese cooking as a flavouring, garnish or for sushi. Sold in thin sheets, plain or toasted (yaki-nori).

NUTMEG a strong and pungent spice ground from the dried nut of an evergreen tree native to Indonesia. Usually found ground but the flavour is more intense from a whole nut, available from spice shops, so it's best to grate your own.

NUTRITIONAL YEAST is deactivated yeast that is a complete protein, as it contains 18 amino acids, including the nine that are essential for good health. It is generally fortified with B12, an important nutrient for vegans that is lacking in a meat-free diet. It is available from health food stores.

QUINOA is the seed of a leafy plant similar to spinach. It has a delicate, slightly nutty taste and chewy texture.

flakes the seeds have been rolled and flattened.

puffed has been steamed until it puffs up.

RICE MALT SYRUP also known as brown rice syrup or rice syrup; is made by cooking brown rice flour with enzymes to break down its starch into sugars from which the water is removed.

STERLISING JARS

It's important the jars be as clean as possible; make sure your hands, the preparation area, tea towels and cloths etc, are clean, too. The aim is to finish sterilising the jars and lids at the same time the preserve is ready to be bottled; the hot preserve should be bottled into hot, dry clean jars. Jars that aren't sterilised properly can cause deterioration of the preserves during storage. Always start with cleaned washed jars and lids, then follow one of these methods:

(1) Put jars and lids through the hottest cycle of a dishwasher without using any detergent.

(2) Lie jars down in a boiler with the lids, cover them with cold water then cover the boiler with a lid. Bring the water to the boil over a high heat and boil the jars for 20 minutes.

(3) Stand jars upright, without touching each other, on a wooden board on the lowest shelf in the oven. Turn the oven to the lowest possible temperature; leave jars to heat for 30 minutes. Remove the jars from the oven or dishwasher with a towel, or from the boiling water with tongs and rubber-gloved hands; the water will evaporate from hot wet jars quite quickly. Stand jars upright and not touching on a wooden board, or a bench covered with a towel to protect and insulate the bench. Fill the jars as directed in the recipe; secure the lids tightly, holding jars firmly with a towel or an oven mitt. Leave at room temperature to cool before storing.

TAHINI a rich, sesame-seed paste, used in most Middle-Eastern cuisines, especially Lebanese, in dips and sauces.

TOFU also called bean curd; an off-white, custard-like product made from the "milk" of crushed soybeans. Comes fresh as soft or firm, and processed as fried or pressed dried sheets. Fresh tofu can be refrigerated in water (changed daily) for up to 4 days.

TURMERIC also called kamin; is a rhizome related to galangal and ginger. Must be grated or pounded to release its acrid aroma and pungent flavour. Known for the golden colour it imparts, fresh turmeric can be substituted with the more commonly found dried powder.

VANILLA

bean long, thin pod from a tropical golden orchid; the minuscule black seeds inside the bean impart a luscious flavour in baking and desserts.

extract obtained from vanilla beans infused in water; a non-alcoholic version of essence.

paste made from vanilla beans and contains real seeds. Is highly concentrated: 1 teaspoon replaces a whole vanilla bean. Found in most supermarkets in the baking section.

VINEGAR

balsamic made from the juice of Trebbiano grapes; it is a deep rich brown colour with a sweet and sour flavour.

cider made from fermented apples.

wine based on red wine.

YEAST (dried and fresh), a raising agent used in dough making. Granular (7g sachets) and fresh compressed (20g blocks) yeast can almost always be substituted for the other.

CONVERSION CHART

MEASURES

One Australian metric measuring cup holds approximately 250ml; one Australian metric tablespoon holds 20ml; one Australian metric teaspoon holds 5ml.

The difference between one country's measuring cups and another's is within a two- or three-teaspoon variance, and will not affect your cooking results. North America, New Zealand and the United Kingdom use a 15ml tablespoon.

All cup and spoon measurements are level. The most accurate way of measuring dry ingredients is to weigh them. When measuring liquids, use a clear glass or plastic jug with the metric markings.

The imperial measurements used in these recipes are approximate only. Measurements for cake pans are approximate only. Using same-shaped cake pans of a similar size should not affect the outcome of your baking. We measure the inside top of the cake pan to determine sizes.

We use large eggs with an average weight of 60g.

DRY MEASURES

METRIC	IMPERIAL
15G	½OZ
30G	1OZ
60G	2OZ
90G	3OZ
125G	4OZ (¼LB)
155G	5OZ
185G	6OZ
220G	7OZ
250G	8OZ (½LB)
280G	9OZ
315G	10OZ
345G	11OZ
375G	12OZ (¾LB)
410G	13OZ
440G	14OZ
470G	15OZ
500G	16OZ (1LB)
750G	24OZ (1½LB)
1KG	32OZ (2LB)

LIQUID MEASURES

METRIC	IMPERIAL
30ML	1 FLUID OZ
60ML	2 FLUID OZ
100ML	3 FLUID OZ
125ML	4 FLUID OZ
150ML	5 FLUID OZ
190ML	6 FLUID OZ
250ML	8 FLUID OZ
300ML	10 FLUID OZ
500ML	16 FLUID OZ
600ML	20 FLUID OZ
1000ML (1 LITRE)	1¾ PINTS

LENGTH MEASURES

METRIC	IMPERIAL
3MM	⅛IN
6MM	¼IN
1CM	½IN
2CM	¾IN
2.5CM	1IN
5CM	2IN
6CM	2½IN
8CM	3IN
10CM	4IN
13CM	5IN
15CM	6IN
18CM	7IN
20CM	8IN
22CM	9IN
25CM	10IN
28CM	11IN
30CM	12IN (1FT)

OVEN TEMPERATURES

The oven temperatures in this book are for conventional ovens; if you have a fan-forced oven, decrease the temperature by 10-20 degrees.

	°C (Celsius)	°F (Fahrenheit)
VERY SLOW	120	250
SLOW	150	300
MODERATELY SLOW	160	325
MODERATE	180	350
MODERATELY HOT	200	400
HOT	220	425
VERY HOT	240	475

INDEX

A

affogato, vietnamese-style
  coconut 198
amaranth porridge, ayurvedic 36
avocado
  avocado, goat's cheese &
    pistachio dukkah topping 77
  dressing 104
  smashed avocado, kimchi &
    seeds topping 77

B

banana
  banana & cinnamon pikelets
    with pan-fried granola 23
  banana & tahini hunger buster
    31
  confetti banana & tahini
    pudding 145
beef
  beef bone broth, slow-cooker
    61
  pho, zucchini noodle 87
beetroot
  beetroot, coconut & seed salad
    with snapper 116
  beetroot & buckwheat risotto
    with goat's curd 84
  beetroot & cacao pancakes with
    raspberry chia jam 12
  kefir water soda 50
  peanut butter & beetroot
    hummus 153
berry
  berry & fig weekend brekkie
    pudding 32
  berrylicious mousse 146
    crumble 205
  kombucha berry jellies with
    cinnamon-cashew ice-cream 177
  purple crush pie 202
  roasted berry frozen yoghurt
    layer cake 193
big beautiful breakfast bowl 20
bircher, cherry, ginger & chia
  43
blackberry, apple & almond bran
  muffins 165
blueberry
  blueberry, orange & oat hunger
    buster 31
  blueberry lemon cheesecake,
    raw 220

bone broth smoothies
  mango, maple & mesquite 16
  raspberry & cacao 16
bountiful bars 137
bread, cheesy parsnip teff 74
breakfast bowl, big beautiful 20
broad beans
  loads-in-one goodness smash 70
broths
  beef bone, slow-cooker 61
  chicken 61
  fish 61
  vegetable 61
bruschetta, strawberry, ricotta
  & basil with bitter honey 28

C

cacao
  cacao bombs with passionfruit
    130
  coating 137
cake
  blueberry lemon cheesecake,
    raw 220
  choc-peanut cake, raw 219
  citrus, orange blossom & bean
    229
  gingerbread apple cupcakes,
    raw 216
  pear cheesecake, spiced 215
  raw carrot, with coconut
    'cream cheese' frosting 185
  raw chocolate jaffa 211
  roasted berry frozen yoghurt
    layer cake 193
caramel 189, 219
  salted caramel sauce 81
  sauce 181
carrot
  raw cake, with coconut 'cream
    cheese' frosting 185
  taco shells with chipotle pork
    95
cashew cream cheese 158
cauliflower bechamel 99
chai mix, dandelion sticky 58
cheese
  cheesy parsnip teff bread 74
  smoked 'cheese' spread 66
cherry, ginger & chia bircher 43
chia
  raspberry chia jam 12, 53, 162
  stonefruit & passionfruit chia
    jam, instant 57

(chia continued)
  turmeric chia breakfast
    puddings 24
chicken
  broth 61
  chicken noodle soup, instant
    flu-helper 138
  ginger chicken with raw citrus
    ribbon salad 112
  quinoa & brown rice chicken
    congee 91
  super greens chicken 104
chilli sauce, no-nasties 69
chocolate
  biscuits 46
  choc chip cookie dough, raw 157
  choc-dipped orange slices 211
  choc-peanut cake, raw 219
  choc-peanut mylkshake 225
  chocolate caramel good times
    181
  chocolate hazelnut slice 178
  chocolate jaffa cake, raw 211
  dark chocolate cherry fudge
    cookies, secret-ingredient 233
  ganache 178, 211
  granita 212
  matcha choc pops 201
  peppermint bites 230
  rawtella pie 190
  sauce 194, 225
  tropical choc-dipped fruit 182
citrus
  cheesecake slice, raw 207
  citrus, orange blossom & bean
    cake 229
coconut
  affogato, vietnamese-style 198
  beetroot, coconut & seed salad
    with snapper 116
  bountiful bars 137
  cheat's coconut ice-cream 198
  coconut & vanilla ice-cream
    sandwiches 46
  coconut-blackberry whip 165
  coconut nam jim 96
  coconut sticky rice ice-cream
    with mango 186
  coconut sundae with caramel
    popcorn 194
  herby pea & coconut soup,
    15-minute 154
  meringues 173
coffee & coconut hunger buster 31

congee, quinoa & brown rice
  chicken 91
cookies
  cookies & cream slice, raw 226
  dark chocolate cherry fudge
    cookies, secret-ingredient 233
  milky tea cookie sandwich 208
  PB & J chickpea 53
  raw choc chip cookie dough 157
  strawberry cream, raw 197
coriander dosa 123
crackers, rosemary & cacao 65
crispbreads, seed & veggie pulp
  149
crumble
  berry 205
  cacoa nib & coconut topping 205
  ginger & spice topping 205
  orange & poppy seed topping 205
  seeds of life topping 205
curry, potato, spinach &
  chickpea, with coriander dosa
  123

daily greens greenola 15
dandelion sticky chai mix 58
dill pickle popcorn 142
dipping sauce, sesame ginger 49
doughnuts, peaches & cream 174

eggplant
  eggplant & zucchini lasagne 99
  spicy eggplant shakshuka 111

fish
  beetroot, coconut & seed salad
    with snapper 116
  broth 61
  fish & fennel stew 120
  fritters, pea & kale with
    hot-smoked salmon 27
  hawaiian poke with brown rice
    88
  roast salmon with spiced
    lentils & dill yoghurt 119
fries, healthy veggie 129
fritters, pea & kale with
  hot-smoked salmon 27
fruit, tropical choc-dipped 182
fudge, frozen tahini, black
  sesame & coconut 126

ginger beer, pineapple 62
ginger chicken with raw citrus
  ribbon salad 112
gingerbread apple cupcakes, raw
  216
goodness smash, loads-in-one 70
granita
  chocolate 212
  orange-pomegranate 212
granola
  daily greens greenola 15
  pan-fried 23
green apple & spirulina kefir
  water soda 50
green goodness shakshuka 111
guacamole, super-food 129

hawaiian poke with brown rice 88
honey
  bitter 28
  honey, macadamia & rosemary
    shortbread 141
  labneh, spiced honey 216
hummus, peanut butter & beetroot
  153
hunger busters
  banana & tahini 31
  blueberry, orange & oat 31
  coffee & coconut 31
  five-minute 31

ice-cream
  cinnamon-cashew 177
  coconut, cheat's 198
  coconut sticky rice, with
    mango 186
ice-cream sandwiches, coconut &
  vanilla 46

jellies, kombucha berry with
  cinnamon-cashew ice-cream 177

kale
  chips with sesame & coriander
    133
  fritters, pea & kale with
    hot-smoked salmon 27

keep-on-going mix, spicy 166
kefir soda, water 50
  beetroot 50
  fresh turmeric & ginger 50
  green apple & spirulina 50
  pineapple & passionfruit 50
  raspberry 50
key lime tartlets 170
kitchari, red lentil 35
kombucha berry jellies with
  cinnamon-cashew ice-cream 177

labneh, spiced honey 216
lamb & walnut pittas with
  turkish salad 115
lamingtons, raw 162
lasagne, eggplant & zucchini 99
latte shake 225
lemon
  blueberry lemon cheesecake,
    raw 220
  lemon meringue pie 173
lime, key, tartlets 170

mango, maple & mesquite smoothie
  16
matcha choc pops 201
mayonnaise, vegan 78
meringue
  coconut meringues 173
  lemon meringue pie 173
milky tea cookie sandwich 208
mousse, berrylicious 146
muffins, blackberry, apple &
  almond bran 165
mushroom & kale pot pies, creamy
  107
mylk
  choc-peanut mylkshake 225
  classic vanilla 223
  latte shake 225
  strawberry 225

no-fry-stir-fry with coconut
  nam jim 96
nougat 219

orange
  orange-pomegranate granita 212
  slices, choc-dipped 211

P

pancakes
banana & cinnamon pikelets
with pan-fried granola 23
beetroot & cacao with
raspberry chia jam 12
papaya power bowl 39
passionfruit
cacao bombs with passionfruit
130
pineapple & passionfruit kefir
water soda 50
stonefruit & passionfruit chia
jam, instant 57
pastry, spelt 107
pea
herby pea & coconut soup,
15-minute 154
pea & kale fritters with
hot-smoked salmon 27
pea, miso & mint rice paper
rolls 134
peanut butter
peanut butter & beetroot
hummus 153
PB & J chickpea cookies 53
pear cheesecake, spiced 215
pecans & almonds, powdered with
rosemary 161
peppermint bites 230
pies
creamy mushroom & kale pot
107
lemon meringue 173
purple crush 202
rawtella 190
pineapple
pineapple & passionfruit kefir
water soda 50
pineapple ginger beer 62
pitta bread crisps 153
popcorn, dill pickle 142
popsicles
chocolate caramel good times
181
matcha choc pops 201
pork, carrot taco shells with
chipotle 95
porridge
ayurvedic amaranth 36
warming quinoa 19
potato, spinach & chickpea curry
with coriander dosa 123
powered pecans & almonds with
rosemary 161

puddings
berry & fig weekend brekkie 32
confetti banana & tahini 145
turmeric chia breakfast 24

Q

quinoa
porridge, warming 19
quinoa & brown rice chicken
congee 91

R

raw slaw salad with pumpernickel
crumbs 150
red lentil kitchari 35
rice paper rolls, pea, miso &
mint 134
risotto, beetroot & buckwheat
with goat's curd 84
rosemary & cacao crackers 65

S

salad
beetroot, coconut & seed salad
with snapper 116
ginger chicken with raw citrus
ribbon salad 112
jars, simple satay 103
raw slaw salad with
pumpernickel crumbs 150
super greens chicken 104
turkish 115
salmon, roast with spiced
lentils & dill yoghurt 119
salted caramel sauce 81
satay salad jars, simple 103
sauerkraut
golden 54
red 54
sesame ginger dipping sauce 49
shakshuka
basic 108
green goodness 111
spicy eggplant 111
white bean with avocado 111
shortbread, honey, macadamia &
rosemary 141
slice
chocolate hazelnut 178
citrus cheesecake slice, raw
207
raw cookies & cream 226
smoothies
mango, maple & mesquite 16
raspberry & cacao 16

soups
chicken noodle soup, instant
flu-helper 138
herby pea & coconut, 15-minute
154
zucchini noodle beef pho 87
'spaghetti' & 'meatballs' 100
spreads
seed, date & tahini 73
smoked 'cheese' 66
stew, fish & fennel 120
stonefruit & passionfruit chia
jam, instant 57
sundae, coconut with caramel
popcorn 194

T

taco shells with chipotle pork,
carrot 95
tahini
confetti banana & tahini
pudding 145
dressing 20
frozen tahini, black sesame &
coconut fudge 126
tartlets, key lime 170
teff
cheat's teff flatbread with
cashew cream cheese 158
cheesy parsnip bread 74
tofu bacon blat 92
tomato, bacon & egg cups,
za'atar-roasted 40
twicker bars, raw 189

V

vegan mayonnaise 78
vegetable broth 61

W

wasabi puffs 104
white bean shakshuka with
avocado 111

Z

za'atar-roasted tomato, bacon &
egg cups 40
zucchini
eggplant & zucchini lasagne 99
noodle beef pho 87